Welcome to

Suzy Spoon's

VEGETARIAN
KITCHEN

I'd like to dedicate this book to Lina Finch, my dear grandma.
I wish she was here to see it.

Welcome to

Suzy Spoon's
VEGETARIAN
KITCHEN

plum. Pan Macmillan Australia

Suzy's

Contents

Hello

> *I really love food.*
> *I'm one of those people*
> *who will commute to the other*
> *side of a city for one special*
> *meal or ingredient.*

When I travel, my entire itinerary is built around places to eat and amazing food producers I want to meet. I love discovering ingredients I've never heard of before and learning new recipes from people I meet along the way. On a recent trip to Turkey, my partner and I were lucky enough to stay with a good friend who is a skilled vegetarian chef, and she showed us all the best vegetarian food in Istanbul. On our last day she took us to a cosy little cafe along the Bosphorus, on the Anatolian side of the city, where she ordered stuffed eggplants called *kuru dolma*. These are rehydrated dried eggplants stuffed with rice and tomato, and they are one of the most delicious things I have ever eaten. I've tried to replicate the recipe many times, but dried eggplants are difficult to get in Australia. Instead, I'm planning my next trip to Turkey because I can't stop thinking about them!

I grew up in country NSW but I have Austrian heritage, so my family ate a lot of European food, like schnitzel, dumplings, red cabbage, goulash and cabanossi. Like most people in my community in the 1970s, I'd never heard of tofu or tempeh. A lot of my cooking is influenced by my Austrian grandma, who taught me to cook. I would sit on a stool in her kitchen and watch her make delicious Austrian specialties like apple strudel. I'd watch in awe as she turned a huge ball of pastry into a paper-thin circle a metre in diameter with her masterful hands. I remember one time when her back was turned, I reached over and touched the paper-thin pastry with my sticky little fingers and tore a big hole in it. I didn't get in trouble, though – she told me she had done the same thing when *she* was a little girl making strudel with her mother.

My childhood was spent living on farms, so I witnessed the everyday farming activities such as the slaughter, skinning and gutting of cows, sheep and rabbits on numerous occasions, but it seemed like quite a natural part of life. But when I was in third grade, Mrs Clark took us on an excursion to an abattoir, where I was quite shocked and upset by the things I saw. And that was when I first started to think about eating animals, and whether it was the right thing for me.

When I was 16, I went to stay on a chicken broiler farm for a short time in New Zealand. The chicks were very cute when they went into the massive sheds, but they grew fast and the sheds quickly became overcrowded. Some birds couldn't move to get to the food or water and the conditions became horrendous. It moved me so much that I gave up eating meat.

I spent many years vegan and, although I'm not vegan now, I still cook mainly vegan food at home as I believe that a vegetable protein–based diet is better for our health and more sustainable for our planet. If you are unfamiliar with the term vegan, it refers to a vegetarian who doesn't eat any eggs, dairy, honey or any animal-derived products at all. I have two beautiful chickens at home named Marilyn and Bob, who are the queens of my yard. And I eat their eggs, which is the main reason I'm not vegan.

Home economics seemed a bit dreary when I was in high school and I wasn't interested in knowing how to make corned beef and white sauce, so I didn't care for cooking much back then. When I left school I had a few different jobs – as an assistant in a production company, waitress, house painter and child care worker. Then one day, I heard about a little sandwich shop for sale in Newtown and I went for it. I'd never really cooked before, but I learnt on the job.

I turned that sandwich shop into my first cafe – MacDonnas – and it was there that my passion for creating new recipes and experimenting with unusual ingredients was born. I ran MacDonnas for four years and it is well remembered by long-term locals.

I was working in a cafe when I heard that the latest *Star Wars* film was being made at Fox Studios in Sydney, and the set-building department was hiring crew. I was sick of cooking bacon and eggs and I'd had some experience painting houses, so I applied. I worked in film and television for the next 10 years, in the set-building and art departments.

But I never lost my passion for cooking. In my spare time I made cooking shows with friends. The first was called *Cooking Cleverly with Beverly*, and screened on community TV. The other was a show called *The Iron-Deficient Chef*, which was a series of webisodes on YouTube.

It was well known among my film and television colleagues that vegetarian cooking was one of my great passions. Almost everyone on *Home and Away* has had to taste test a vegetarian sausage at some point. And when Tobey Maguire's personal assistant needed to find a vegan chef for Toby while he was in Sydney filming *The Great Gatsby*, he thought of me. Tobey loved my homemade sausages, burger patties and seitan schnitzels, and so I had the idea to develop a range of vegetarian products and start selling them at the local markets.

I had already been experimenting with making vegan sausages and faux meat products for many years. On a trip to Vienna with my family once, my mum and I had come across a stall selling vegan crumbed schnitzels. They were delicious. I ate one on the spot and bought five more to take back to my hotel, where I lived on them for the rest of our trip. I'd never tasted anything like that before, and as soon as I got home I began experimenting with making seitan schnitzel.

My products were a hit at the markets and I now have my very own vegetarian butcher's shop. We make four different flavours of vegan sausages by hand, as well as burger patties, seitan, bolognese and smoky rashers (faux bacon). And our best seller is – you guessed it – my Vienna-style crumbed schnitzel.

I also have a healthy obsession with vegetables, and I hope to inspire you with this book to cook and eat more vegetables – whether you're vegetarian or not. I think a lot of people are looking for new and interesting ways to incorporate more veggies into their diet, and hopefully I can help with that!

I hope that there is something for everyone in this book. It is a collection of recipes that I have been working on and compiling for over 10 years, and is a real celebration of plant-based ingredients. I have tried to create recipes that are exciting, delicious and nourishing; food that fills you up, looks fabulous, is simple to prepare and can be enjoyed by vegetarians, vegans and meat-eaters alike. I believe vegetarian dishes can easily be the focal point of a meal, and it's the combination of fresh ingredients, interesting textures and wonderful flavours that make my recipes so enticing. I hope you enjoy this book. I am proud to share it with you.

 Cook's

Notes

This is primarily a vegetarian cookbook, but most of my recipes can be made vegan-friendly simply by using dairy alternatives or egg replacer. Supermarkets and health food shops stock some great alternatives for milk, cheese, cream cheese, sour cream and yoghurt. Even though these products tend to be highly processed, they're fun to use every now and again, and I love how they allow me to add more variety to my recipes.

Ingredients

Delicious, healthy meals rely on the freshest ingredients. Here are some tips on sourcing and preparing the ingredients for the recipes in this book.

VEGETABLES AND FRUIT

Freshness is paramount for vegetables and fruit, and locally produced seasonal produce is better for us and for the planet. I let my menus be led by their ingredients – if I see an amazing bunch of kale at the local farmers market, I'll take it home and build a meal around it (such as veggie sausages with kale salad). I think this works much better than finding a recipe for mulberry pie and going on a search for mulberries only to find they are $12 a punnet because they've been flown here from Argentina. When you are following the recipes in this book assume that all vegetables and fruits are washed before you peel or cut them.

DAIRY PRODUCTS

I don't use dairy products, but I've included them in some recipes in this book to make it user-friendly for non-vegans. If you *are* vegan or lactose-intolerant, you will no doubt be adept at replacing cow's milk with nut milk or soy milk, and butter with dairy-free spread. Milks made from brown rice, oats and almonds are great, so I've included recipes for each of these (see pages 234–7). I love pastry, so you'll find several recipes for pies and tarts that include instructions on how to make pastry from scratch using butter or dairy-free spread. If you don't have time to make your own there is no shame in using frozen pastry. However, if you are going to make your own, always use chilled butter or dairy-free spread (you don't want to melt the fat until the pastry is in the oven – it's a chemistry thing).

EGGS

I rarely use eggs, but some of the recipes in this book include them. Vegans can easily substitute the eggs with one of the many egg replacers on the market, such as Orgran No Egg, which can be found in most supermarkets and all good health food stores. If you are going to use eggs I urge you make the effort to use free-range ones. Buying free-range eggs sends the message to supermarkets that people want food sourced with care and compassion. Genuine free-range eggs will cost a bit more, because farmers have a bigger outlay for grassy, safe yards, bigger sheds and better, cleaner conditions for their animals.

LEGUMES

Beans and lentils are delicious and one of the best sources of plant protein. They are high in dietary and soluble fibre so they can help lower cholesterol. When preparing dried legumes always rinse them in water before cooking. Most of my legume recipes include instructions for preparing them from scratch, but it's also completely fine to use tinned ones.

GARLIC

Most of my recipes call for garlic to be minced, and for this you can use a garlic crusher or micro plane (which is a fine grater). Minced garlic cooks very quickly so to avoid a bitter burnt flavour always add it with other ingredients or cook it only for a few seconds. Depending on the dish, I sometimes finely chop it or smash it (sprinkle it with salt and press it with the flat blade of a knife).

CHILLIES

When I say 'small chilli' I mean bird's eye chillies, which are very hot. The long red ones are usually cayenne chillies, which are a lot milder. When I ask for chillies to be deseeded (to reduce their heat), slice them lengthways and scrape out the seeds with the tip of the knife. Wash your hands well after handling chillies as they can cause irritation to the eyes and nose.

VEGETABLE OILS

Olive oil tastes great and is really healthy too. I use it for salads and for sautéing at low temperatures. (I don't usually cook it at high temperatures because it has a low smoke point and becomes unstable.) Feel free to substitute your favourite oils. For frying, I use rice bran or canola oil. I never buy oil labelled 'vegetable oil' because it's a blend of many types of oil and I can never be sure what has been used in the blend.

MOCK MEAT/SEITAN

The reason I don't eat meat is because I disagree with modern animal husbandry and factory farming methods, not because I don't like the flavour and texture. So as weird as it might sound, I like to use meat replacements ('mock meat'). Meat alternatives provide a different texture to enjoy and open up possibilities for recreating traditional recipes. Seitan is a meat-like substance made from the protein of wheat flour. Although you can buy ready-made seitan from health food stores and Asian grocery stores, I show you how to to make your own seitan from scratch, both the 'easy way' (using wheat gluten flour – see pages 127, 128, 132, 136 and 141), and the 'hard-but-more-fun way' (using plain flour – see page 138).

TOFU AND TEMPEH

Tofu and tempeh are great sources of protein. Tofu is made by adding a curdling agent to soy milk so that it separates into curds and whey. The curd is pressed to remove the liquid and make either 'silken' or 'firm' tofu. Silken tofu is soft and moist because it hasn't been pressed for long and has retained more of the liquid. It is perfect for desserts, dips and sauces. Firm tofu has been pressed for longer so has a firmer, dryer texture. It is great for salads, sandwiches, barbecues and stir fries. Tempeh is made by cooking soybeans, popping off their husks and adding a powdered culture starter to ferment the beans. The beans are left in a warm place for a day until an edible white mould forms around them. You can try making your own tempeh at home – tempeh culture starter is available online and there are lots of online instructional videos. I've made it a few times, and worked out that the top of my DVD player was the perfect temperature for fermentation.

MISO PASTE

Miso is a fermented soybean paste and I usually use it as a flavour enhancer and seasoning. Dark miso is great for making a broth for cooking seitan and giving foods a rich, salty, umami flavour and a dark brown colouring. White miso is sweeter and not as salty, but still imparts an umami flavour that is hard to obtain any other way. I use it as a base for soups and sauces. And I love it on toast with tahini. Miso paste can be found in supermarkets, health food stores and Asian grocery stores.

SWEETENERS

I love the intense malted flavour of molasses, the syrupy by-product of sugar extraction. Golden syrup is the lightest version of molasses, then there's dark molasses (which is thicker and stronger in taste) and blackstrap molasses (my favourite). Blackstrap molasses is higher in iron and other minerals than the lighter varieties, but the bittersweet flavour might not be for everyone. If you don't like molasses, try brown rice syrup, maple syrup, coconut syrup, coconut sugar, cane sugar or agave. Non-vegans can also use honey.

Equipment

COOK'S KNIFE

A good knife for preparing your veggies is a must. The safest knife is the knife you are used to, and I recommend you get used to a good-quality, heavy-handled knife bought from a homewares store, catering shop or knife shop.

CHEESECLOTH

I've included recipes for making your own non-dairy milks (see pages 234–7) so if you want to make these you'll need some unbleached cheesecloth to strain them. You can also use other cloth as long as it allows liquid to pass through, is clean and is free of chemicals and dyes.

FOOD PROCESSOR

A food processor or blender is important for making pastes, sauces, smoothies and almond milk (see recipe, page 234). A stick blender is good for soups and sauces.

CHOPPING BOARDS

I like a good, sturdy chopping board and use heavy, wooden ones at home. It's good to have a number of chopping boards so you always have a clean one on hand – important for both flavour and good kitchen hygiene.

MORTAR AND PESTLE

A good mortar and pestle is essential in the kitchen. Before I put anything into a food processor I first ask myself whether I could do it in the mortar and pestle. I love the rustic appearance of the results. It's also less fuss, less electricity and less washing up than a food processor.

FRYING PANS

I avoid cheap, nonstick pans. At home I use heavy, cast-iron, enamelled cookware, as I love its nonstick qualities and even heat distribution.

 Suzy's

Breakfasts

Perfect
banana
pancakes

These pancakes taste as good as they look, especially with sliced banana, lemon juice and a dash of maple syrup.

300 g (2 cups) plain flour

2 teaspoons baking powder

¾ teaspoon salt

1 teaspoon sugar

500 ml (2 cups) soy milk

1 teaspoon vanilla extract

dairy-free spread or rice bran oil, to fry

2 bananas, sliced

lemon wedges, to serve

maple syrup, to serve

VEGAN

Sift the flour and baking powder into a large bowl. Stir in the salt and sugar. Whisk in the soy milk, 90 ml of water and vanilla. Cover and rest in the fridge for 20 minutes.

Heat a large frying pan over a medium heat. When hot, add a little dairy-free spread or oil. Pour in ¼ cup of batter and cook for 3–5 minutes on each side, or until golden (this should form a pancake about 15 cm in diameter). Keep warm. Repeat the process until all the batter is used.

Serve the pancakes hot with sliced banana, a squeeze of lemon juice and a drizzle of maple syrup.

Makes 16 pancakes

TIP Beware of maple-flavoured sugar syrup – it's not the same as pure maple syrup, which is collected from maple trees!

Baked strawberry quinoa

Ten years ago I hadn't heard of quinoa, but these days it's hard to miss – and for good reason. It's delicious, versatile and nutritious, being high in iron and amino acids, especially lysine, and I have embraced it with open arms. This dish would also make a lovely dessert, but I've included it here as a spring breakfast – when it's warm enough for strawberries to be fruiting but still cool enough in the mornings to warrant something hot and sustaining.

250 g (1 punnet) strawberries, hulled and quartered

200 g (1 cup) white quinoa, rinsed

1 granny smith apple, peeled, cored and diced

3 tablespoons currants

250 ml (1 cup) apple juice

½ teaspoon ground cinnamon

½ teaspoon ground nutmeg

3 tablespoons slivered almonds, toasted, to serve

milk, to serve

GLUTEN-FREE

Preheat the oven to 180°C. Reserve some strawberries to garnish.

In a small heavy-based baking dish, combine all the ingredients (except the almonds and milk) with 125 ml (½ cup) of water. Cover and bake for 45 minutes, or until the fruit is soft and the quinoa has the consistency of porridge.

Serve hot, topped with the extra strawberries, toasted almonds and milk of your choice.

Serves 2

TIP To toast the almonds, heat a small frying pan over a medium heat. Add the almonds and brown for 5–7 minutes, shaking or stirring them regularly so they don't burn.

Banana toast (for little monkeys)

Keeping young children happy at the table can be tough, but this recipe will do the trick. I created it for my visiting nieces and nephews one morning for breakfast, and had to make a whole new batch once the adults had a taste as well!

3 ripe bananas

250 ml (1 cup) soy milk

1 tablespoon plain flour

1½ teaspoons ground cinnamon

1 teaspoon vanilla extract

2 tablespoons rice bran oil

8 slices of soft wholemeal bread

golden syrup, to serve

VEGAN

Place the bananas in a large bowl and mash well. Add the soy milk and mix gently. Stir in the flour, cinnamon and vanilla until well combined but still a bit lumpy.

Heat 1 tablespoon of the oil in a frying pan over a medium–low heat. Dip one bread slice into the banana mixture and fry for 3–5 minutes on each side until golden brown. (Be careful, the banana can burn very quickly.) Set aside and keep warm. Repeat with the remaining bread slices, frying 1 or 2 at a time depending on the size of your pan, until all the mixture is used, adding extra oil as needed.

Serve hot with a drizzle of golden syrup.

Serves 4

Grilled polenta cakes with lima beans

Polenta (cornmeal) is often forgotten here in Australia, but its vitamins, minerals, fibre and complex carbs make it a super-healthy and scrumptious start to your day. If you prepare the polenta cakes the night before you can make this breakfast in about 20 minutes. They would make a great lunch, too, with a leafy green salad. And you can easily make this gluten-free simply by using gluten-free bread.

170 g (1 cup) polenta

¼ teaspoon salt

120 ml (scant ½ cup) olive oil

1 onion, diced

2 x 400 g cans lima beans, drained and rinsed

1 tablespoon butter

1 tablespoon white miso paste

¼ teaspoon salt

¼ teaspoon freshly ground black pepper

4 slices of bread, toasted

grated parmesan, to serve

TIP To prepare your own beans, soak 1½ cups of dried lima beans or butter beans in 1 litre of water overnight. Drain and rinse. Transfer to a saucepan with 1.25 litres of fresh water and bring to the boil over a medium heat. Boil, uncovered, for 60 minutes, or until tender.

Grease 8 cups in a 12-cup muffin tray.

Pour the polenta into a heavy-based saucepan along with the salt and stir in 750 ml (3 cups) of water. Bring to the boil over a medium heat. Reduce the heat to low, cover and cook for 20 minutes, stirring often. The polenta will thicken and pull away from the sides of the pan when it's ready.

Spoon the polenta into the muffin tray cups to about half full. Place the tray in the fridge for at least 30 minutes until the polenta firms up (overnight is fine).

Heat 3 tablespoons of the olive oil in a heavy-based frying pan over a medium heat. Add the onion and sauté for 5 minutes, or until soft and transparent. Add the beans and butter and sauté for another 5 minutes.

Dissolve the miso paste in 500 ml (2 cups) of water and pour over the beans. Add the salt and pepper. Cook, uncovered, for 20 minutes, or until the liquid has reduced by half.

Meanwhile, remove the polenta cakes from the muffin tray. Heat the remaining 3 tablespoons of oil in a frying pan over a medium heat and fry the polenta cakes for 5–7 minutes on each side until golden brown.

To serve, place a spoonful of beans on a slice of toast and top with the polenta. Sprinkle over some freshly grated parmesan and serve immediately.

Serves 4

Truly amazing homemade crumpets

I'd *love* you to make these! They are, indeed, truly amazing, and much easier than you think. Because the batter has to rest for at least 4 hours, it's a good idea to make it the night before so it's ready to go the next morning. Check that you have a few egg rings before you start (that's how you make them nice and round).

150 ml warm water

1 teaspoon dry yeast

265 g (1¾ cups) plain flour

175 ml soy milk

pinch of salt

1 teaspoon bicarbonate of soda

2–3 tablespoons canola oil, for cooking

dairy-free spread and golden syrup, to serve

VEGAN

Place the warm water in a small bowl and stir in the yeast. Add 150 g (1 cup) of the flour and stir until well combined. Cover the yeast mixture with a clean tea-towel and place in a warm spot for 20 minutes until bubbles form on the surface.

Transfer the yeast mixture to a large bowl. Add the soy milk, salt and bicarbonate of soda and stir well. Fold in the remaining flour. Cover, and rest for at least 4 hours or overnight.

Rub some canola oil on the inside edge of the egg rings to prevent the batter from sticking.

Heat 1 tablespoon of the canola oil in a large frying pan over a medium heat. Place 4 egg rings on the base of the pan. Spoon the batter into each ring (don't overfill). Cook for 3 minutes on each side, or until golden brown (turn them with an egg-lift or spatula). Repeat the process until all the batter has been used.

Cut the hot crumpets in half and spread with dairy-free spread and golden syrup. (You can store any leftovers in a plastic container in the fridge for 2–3 days – just halve them and reheat in the toaster as needed.)

Serves 4–6

Oat and sunflower seed loaf

This flourless loaf is *scarily* healthy! It's high in protein, fibre and omega-3 and has an amazing flavour and texture. Try it for breakfast, spread with avocado, or take it to work for lunch with tomato and rocket. The dough needs to sit for 8–12 hours to allow the linseeds and chia seeds to become gelatinous – this is the secret to binding the ingredients.

125 g (1 cup) sunflower seeds

90 g (½ cup) linseeds

65 g (½ cup) hazelnuts

150 g (1½ cups) rolled oats

2 tablespoons chia seeds

3 tablespoons psyllium husks

1 teaspoon sea salt flakes

3 tablespoons golden syrup

3 tablespoons canola oil

VEGAN

Grease a loaf tin.

Combine all the dry ingredients in a large mixing bowl.

In a smaller bowl whisk together the golden syrup, oil and 350 ml of water. Add the wet ingredients to the dry ingredients and mix to form a wet dough. Wait 5 minutes for the liquid to absorb into the nuts and grains. If the mixture is not binding well, add 1–2 extra teaspoons of water.

Transfer the dough to the loaf tin. Cover and sit it in a draft-free place (not in the fridge) for 8–12 hours.

Preheat the oven to 180°C.

Sprinkle 2 tablespoons of water on top of the loaf. Bake for 35–40 minutes, or until golden brown on top.

Remove from the oven. Run a knife around the edge of the tin. Turn the loaf out onto a cooling rack and leave to cool.

Slice and serve warm, cold or toasted. Store the loaf in a plastic bag or airtight container for 4–5 days.

Makes 1 loaf

Crispy potato and tofu fritters

These delicious fritters can also be made using gluten-free flour. Waxy potatoes such as desirees or pontiacs make the best fritters as they hold together better during the cooking process.

800 g potatoes, peeled and grated

150 g firm tofu, crumbled

3 tablespoons wholemeal flour

½ teaspoon salt

60 ml (¼ cup) rice bran oil

1 avocado, diced

2 tomatoes, diced

freshly ground black pepper

lemon wedges, to serve

VEGAN

Combine the potato, tofu, flour and salt in a large bowl and mix well using a wooden spoon.

Heat the oil in a large heavy-based frying pan over a medium–high heat. Place ¼ cup of the mixture into the pan and flatten slightly to make each fritter. Cook the fritters in batches for 5–7 minutes on each side, or until golden brown and crisp. Drain on paper towel.

Serve hot, topped with the avocado, tomato and a pinch of freshly ground black pepper. Squeeze over some lemon juice.

Serves 4

Sunday morning special

I love a Sunday at home – taking time with breakfast, reading the paper and tending to the veggie garden. This breakfast is the perfect start to such a day, especially if you have guests. The excess basil oil can be stored in the fridge for 2 to 3 weeks and is delicious drizzled over a baked potato or a salad.

4 large portobello or field mushrooms

2 tablespoons olive oil

salt and freshly ground black pepper

30 g (about ¼ bunch) basil, leaves picked

125 ml (½ cup) olive oil

4 slices of sourdough bread

1 garlic clove, peeled and halved

1 avocado, sliced

Chunky Tomato Relish (page 176), to serve

VEGAN

Preheat the oven to 180°C.

De-stem the mushrooms and place them underside-up on a small baking tray. Drizzle with the olive oil. Season with salt and pepper, cover the tray with foil and bake for 35 minutes. Remove the foil and return the tray to the oven for a further 10 minutes.

To make the basil oil, blend the basil and olive oil in a food processor. Add a pinch of salt and process until smooth.

Toast the bread and rub each slice with garlic. Top with sliced avocado, a mushroom, a dollop of relish and 2 tablespoons of basil oil. Season and serve immediately.

Serves 2

Mushroom and tofu scramble

Some people think scrambled tofu is a bit out of fashion, but this delicious little recipe should convince you that it's worth bringing back. It's low in fat and high in protein, vitamin C and iron and is so versatile – you can whip it up as a nourishing breakfast or serve with a baked potato for a quick lunch or dinner.

2 tablespoons olive oil

100 g (1 cup) button mushrooms, diced

4 spring onions, sliced

3 garlic cloves, minced

1 large tomato, diced

250 g firm tofu, crumbled

8 slices of bread, to serve

salt and freshly ground black pepper

VEGAN

Heat the oil in a frying pan over a medium heat. Add the mushrooms and sauté for 5 minutes, or until just beginning to soften. Add the spring onions, garlic and tomato and sauté for 5 minutes, or until softened. Finally, stir in the crumbled tofu and cook for 10 minutes, stirring regularly, until the tofu is moist but not soggy.

Toast the bread and serve each slice topped with the hot mushroom and tofu scramble. Season with salt and freshly ground black pepper.

Serves 4

Quick and easy baked beans

These homemade beans are not only nutritious, but also taste awesome, especially on toast or a baked potato. Store any leftovers in the fridge in an airtight plastic container and you can reheat them for easy meals for a couple of days. This dish can also be cooked in a camp oven in the ground, cowgirl style.

60 ml (¼ cup) olive oil

½ white onion, diced

4 garlic cloves, finely chopped

2 tablespoons white miso paste

4 tomatoes, diced

2 tablespoons tomato paste

½ tablespoon dark brown sugar

1 tablespoon balsamic vinegar

1 clove

2 x 400 g cans cannellini beans, drained and rinsed

¼ teaspoon salt

pinch of freshly ground black pepper

toast, to serve

VEGAN

Preheat the oven to 180°C.

Heat the oil in a small frying pan over a medium heat. Add the onion and sauté for 2–3 minutes, or until soft and brown. Add the garlic and sauté for 20–30 seconds, being careful not to let it burn.

In a heavy-based baking dish (or casserole dish) combine the miso paste with 250 ml (1 cup) of water. Add the tomatoes, tomato paste, sugar, vinegar, clove and sautéed onions and garlic mix well. Add the beans, salt and pepper. Cover with a heavy lid and bake for 30 minutes. Remove the lid and return the dish to the oven to cook for a further 20 minutes, or until the sauce thickens. Remove the clove before serving.

Serve hot on a toasted slice or two of your favourite bread.

Serves 4

TIP If you prefer to prepare your own beans, soak 1½ cups of dried cannellini beans in 1 litres of water overnight. Drain and rinse. Transfer to a saucepan with 1.25 litres of fresh water and bring to the boil over a medium heat. Boil, uncovered, for 90 minutes, or until tender.

Suzy's

Soups

Tomato and silverbeet soup with polenta dumplings

This soup is everything I love about Italian food – simple, fresh ingredients that perfectly complement each other in texture and flavour.

2 tablespoons olive oil, plus extra to serve

1½ onions, chopped

2 fresh bay leaves (or 1 dried)

1 tablespoon chopped oregano leaves

3 large garlic cloves, minced

pinch of ground allspice

1½ tablespoons raw sugar

1 kg tomatoes, diced

2 tablespoons white miso paste

1 kg bunch of silverbeet, stalks removed and leaves sliced

salt and freshly ground black pepper

POLENTA DUMPLINGS

2 tablespoons white miso paste

170 g (1 cup) polenta

1 white onion, finely diced

4 garlic cloves, minced

To make the polenta dumplings, heat 750 ml (3 cups) of water in a large heavy-based saucepan over a medium heat. Stir in the miso paste. When dissolved add the polenta, onion and garlic. Cover and cook for 30 minutes, stirring regularly. (Be careful – hot polenta can spit like a bubbling cauldron of lava!) The polenta is ready when it's really thick and comes away from the sides of the saucepan as you stir it. Remove the pan from the heat and allow to cool slightly.

Line a baking tray with paper.

With wet hands, shape tablespoonfuls of the polenta mixture into 18 round dumplings. Place the dumplings on the tray. Cover with plastic wrap and refrigerate for 30 minutes.

To make the soup, heat the oil in a large saucepan or stockpot over a medium heat. Add the onion and bay leaves and sauté until the onion is translucent. Stir in the oregano, garlic, allspice and sugar and sauté for 2 minutes. Add the tomatoes, miso paste and 1.5 litres of water and bring to a high simmer. Reduce the heat, cover and simmer gently for 30 minutes, stirring occasionally. Add the polenta dumplings and silverbeet and cook for 3–5 minutes, or until the silverbeet is wilted.

Ladle the soup into serving bowls, making sure you distribute the silverbeet and dumplings evenly. Drizzle with olive oil and season to taste. Serve immediately.

Serves 6

VEGAN

Ginger–miso soup with yuba and tofu

Yuba (tofu skin) has a chewy texture, yet is soft and delicate so is great to experiment with in cooking. It's actually a by-product of soy milk production and comes in sheets or dried sticks. You should be able to find it in Asian grocery stores and some health food stores. If you've never used yuba, this soup is a great way to try it.

8 small Swiss brown mushrooms, halved

3 cm piece of ginger, peeled and sliced

100 g yuba sticks, rinsed in cold water

70 g (¼ cup) dark miso paste

100 g firm tofu, cut into 1 cm cubes

2 spring onions, sliced

sprigs of coriander

1 long red chilli, finely sliced

VEGAN

Place the mushrooms and ginger in a large saucepan or stockpot with 2 litres of water. Break the yuba into finger-length pieces and add them to the water. Bring to the boil, covered, over a medium–high heat. Reduce the heat then simmer, uncovered, for 20 minutes.

Remove a cupful of the broth, add the miso paste and stir gently to dissolve. Pour the miso mixture back into the pan along with the tofu. Stir well and remove from the heat.

Place a small handful of spring onion in each serving bowl, pour over the soup and garnish with coriander sprigs and slices of chilli. Serve immediately.

Serves 4

Buckwheat noodle and mushroom soup

Making your own noodles is a lot of fun, and much easier than you think. Your friends and family will be so impressed with your culinary prowess when they taste this soup and learn that you made the buckwheat noodles yourself!

85 g (½ cup) buckwheat flour

75 g (½ cup) plain flour

¼ teaspoon salt

100 ml olive oil

4 tablespoons boiling water

1 onion, finely diced

4 garlic cloves, minced

250 g oyster mushrooms, larger ones halved

120 g (3 cups loosely packed) baby spinach leaves

2 tablespoons dark miso paste

3 spring onions, cut diagonally into 5 cm lengths, to garnish

1 long red chilli, deseeded and finely sliced, to garnish

sprigs of coriander, to garnish

VEGAN

To make the noodles, sift the flours and salt into a mixing bowl. Make a well in the centre and pour in 3 tablespoons of the oil and the boiling water. Place a wooden spoon in the centre of the well and stir, beginning with little circles, easing the flour in from the sides until you have a stiff dough. Knead the dough in the bowl and form into a ball.

Sprinkle a smooth, clean surface with flour. Turn the dough out onto the floured surface and knead gently and lovingly for 5 minutes until smooth and velvety. Use a rolling pin to roll the dough out as thinly as possible. With a sharp knife slice the dough into long noodles, 1 cm wide. Dust with buckwheat flour so they don't stick together. Transfer to a plate, cover and refrigerate for 20 minutes.

Heat the remaining 2 tablespoons of oil in a large saucepan over a medium heat and sauté the onion for 3 minutes, or until translucent. Add the garlic, mushrooms and spinach and sauté for 2 minutes. In a small bowl dissolve the miso paste in 250 ml (1 cup) of water and add to the pan along with another 750 ml (3 cups) of water. Bring the soup to the boil. Add the noodles and cook for 3–4 minutes.

Ladle the soup into serving bowls and garnish with the spring onions, chilli and coriander sprigs.

Serves 4

Green split pea and smoked tofu soup

This is a seriously good soup that every vegetarian and vegan should have in their repertoire. It is flavoursome, nourishing, filling and really easy to make. I can guarantee it will become a staple in your household. Smoked tofu is available in most health food stores and some supermarkets and Asian grocery stores.

60 ml (¼ cup) olive oil

2 large onions, diced

200 g (1 cup) green split peas, rinsed

1 tablespoon salt

2 carrots, chopped

100 g smoked tofu, cut into 5 mm cubes

crusty bread, to serve

VEGAN

Heat the oil in a heavy-based saucepan over a medium heat. Add the onion and sauté for 5 minutes, or until soft and golden. Add the green split peas and sauté for a further 3 minutes, stirring regularly. Add the salt along with 1.5 litres of water. Reduce the heat to medium–low and cook, uncovered, for 20 minutes, stirring often. Add the carrot and cook for a further 20 minutes, continuing to stir regularly (you'll notice the peas beginning to soften).

Add the tofu and cook for another 15 minutes, or until all the peas have disintegrated and the soup is thick and smooth.

Serve hot with some crusty bread.

Serves 4

Warming lentil soup

This lentil soup has the most delicious flavour, created from a subtle combination of fresh herbs and delicate spices. I like to use red lentils because they cook quickly and go a lovely yellow/orange colour when cooked, but you can use other types of lentils or even tinned lentils if you are in a hurry. If you use tinned lentils, reduce the cooking time to 15 minutes.

3 tablespoons olive oil

1 onion, diced

2 cups red lentils, rinsed

2 garlic cloves, finely chopped, plus an extra clove for the toast

¼ teaspoon ground cinnamon

½ teaspoon ground cumin

1 clove

½ teaspoon chopped thyme leaves

½ teaspoon chopped oregano leaves

salt and freshly ground black pepper

3 tablespoons red miso paste

4 slices of your favourite bread, to serve

VEGAN

Heat the oil in a large, heavy-based saucepan or stockpot over a medium heat and sauté the onion for 5 minutes, or until soft and golden. Stir in the lentils, finely chopped garlic, cinnamon, cumin, clove, thyme and oregano and season with salt and pepper.

In a large jug, dissolve the miso paste in 750 ml (3 cups) of water. Add the miso water to the pan, stirring to combine, and slowly bring to the boil. Reduce the heat and simmer for 1 hour, or until the lentils are soft.

Just before the soup is ready, toast the bread. Peel and halve the remaining clove of garlic and rub each slice of toast with the cut surface of garlic. Place a slice of toast in the base of each serving bowl. Pour over the soup and serve immediately.

Serves 4

Baked mushroom soup

Baking the mushrooms really adds to the earthy flavour of this amazing soup. Be sure to use a hand-held blender to mash the potato so you get the full, silky creaminess.

600 g field or portobello mushrooms

200 g (2 large) waxy potatoes (desiree or pontiac)

3 tablespoons olive oil

1 large onion, diced

4 garlic cloves, minced

1 tablespoon salt

¼ teaspoon freshly ground black pepper

crusty bread, to serve

VEGAN

Preheat the oven to 180°C. Grease a couple of baking trays.

De-stem the mushrooms and place upside down on the trays. Bake for 30 minutes, or until they are soft and begin to caramelise around the edges. Remove from the oven and roughly chop. Place in a food processor and pulse for 30 seconds until pureed. Set aside.

Meanwhile, wash, peel and halve the potatoes and place in a saucepan of water (enough to cover). Bring to the boil over a medium heat. Cook at a rolling boil for 15 minutes, or until soft (test with a skewer). Drain. Transfer to a large bowl and use a hand-held blender to mash the potato until it is smooth and almost sticky.

Heat the olive oil in a large saucepan over a medium heat. Sauté the onion for 3–5 minutes, or until translucent. Add 1 litre (4 cups) of water along with the garlic, salt and pepper and simmer for 15–20 minutes. Add the pureed mushrooms and mashed potato. Cook the soup, uncovered, for 20 minutes, stirring regularly.

Serve hot with crusty bread.

Serves 4

The tastiest laksa

This laksa has beautifully balanced flavours yet packs a punch. Feel free to deseed the chillies if you prefer less heat, or to add even more chilli if you love a bit of fire in your belly! I love the smooth, silky texture of fresh white rice noodles, but you can use dried ones if you prefer.

1 cinnamon stick

8 kaffir lime leaves

1 carrot, cut into batons

120 g (2 cups) broccoli florets

250 g (2 cups) cauliflower florets

4 button mushrooms, sliced

250 g fried tofu puffs

2 × 400 ml cans coconut milk

200 g flat white rice noodles

2 handfuls bean sprouts

mint leaves, to serve

1 red chilli, sliced, to serve

lime wedges, to serve

LAKSA PASTE

juice of 2 limes

8 basil leaves

½ bunch of coriander, washed and stems retained

2 spring onions, sliced

2 lemongrass stems, white part only, finely chopped

4 cm piece of ginger, peeled

5 garlic cloves, peeled

2 tablespoons tomato paste

3 tablespoons brown sugar

3 tablespoons soy sauce

3 small red chillies, diced

1 tablespoon ground cumin

1 tablespoon ground coriander

1 tablespoon savoury yeast flakes

To make the laksa paste, combine all the ingredients in a food processor and process until smooth.

Heat a heavy-based saucepan over a medium–low heat. Add the paste, cover and cook, stirring occasionally, for 10–15 minutes, or until the paste darkens and the aroma becomes intense.

Uncover the pan and add the cinnamon stick, kaffir lime leaves, vegetables, mushrooms and tofu. Stir well to coat the vegetables. Add the coconut milk, cover and cook a further 20 minutes.

Meanwhile, in a large bowl, soak the noodles in 750 ml (3 cups) of boiling water for 10 minutes, or until soft and separated. Drain.

To serve, place a handful of noodles into each bowl and top with a pile of fresh bean sprouts. Ladle over the hot laksa and garnish with mint leaves, chilli slices and a squeeze of lime juice.

Serves 4

GLUTEN-FREE

VEGAN

Tofu dumplings in clear mushroom soup

I love the combination of simple ingredients and delicate flavours in this soup, and I especially love the dumplings! Make sure you use either home-made vegetable stock or a good-quality store-bought variety – it makes all the difference.

DUMPLINGS

200 g (2 large) pontiac or desiree potatoes

300 g firm tofu, crumbled

2 tablespoons plain flour

30 g (1 cup) flat-leaf parsley leaves, roughly chopped

½ teaspoon thyme leaves

1 teaspoon salt

½ teaspoon freshly ground black pepper

SOUP

1 teaspoon coriander seeds

1 litre (4 cups) vegetable stock

4 cm piece of ginger, peeled and minced

1 garlic clove, minced

2 coriander stems, leaves picked, roots and stalks cleaned and retained

8 button mushrooms, diced

salt and freshly ground black pepper

Wash, peel and grate the potatoes into a colander. Squish the potato against the sides of the colander with the back of a wooden spoon to drain excess liquid.

Place the grated potato, tofu, flour, parsley, thyme, salt and pepper in a food processor and process for 30 seconds, or until combined. (The mixture should be moist but not sloppy.) Wet your hands and shape the mixture into tablespoon-sized dumplings. Pop them on a plate and set aside (you'll make about 20).

Toast the coriander seeds in a small frying pan over a medium heat for 3 minutes, or until aromatic. Remove from the heat. Cool slightly before crushing the seeds using a mortar and pestle.

Pour the stock into a large saucepan. Add the crushed coriander seeds, ginger, garlic and coriander roots and stems (the leaves are for serving). Bring to the boil over a medium–high heat then reduce the heat to low and simmer for 30 minutes. Add the mushrooms and dumplings. Return the soup to the boil, then reduce the heat and simmer for a further 15 minutes.

Ladle into serving bowls, sprinkle with coriander leaves and season to taste with salt and pepper.

Serves 4

VEGAN

Suzy's

Salads

Spiced tofu and beetroot salad

The spiced tofu in this dish is packed with intense flavours and is great on sandwiches, in wraps or served as a side. Here I've combined it with colourful beetroot to create a salad that will quite simply blow you away!

750 ml (3 cups) olive oil

1 teaspoon black mustard seeds

1 teaspoon chilli flakes

2 teaspoons fennel seeds

1 teaspoon ground coriander

1 teaspoon ground cumin

3 large beetroots, trimmed

1 teaspoon ground turmeric

500 g firm tofu, cut into 1 cm cubes

100 g (2 cups firmly packed) baby spinach leaves

1½ tablespoons caramelised balsamic vinegar

GLUTEN-FREE

VEGAN

Heat the oil and mustard seeds in a heavy-based frying pan over a medium–low heat. Add the chilli flakes and fennel seeds. Sauté for 2–3 minutes, or until the mustard seeds start to pop and you smell a lovely aroma. Add the coriander and cumin and mix through. Remove from the heat and set aside to cool.

Meanwhile, heat 2 litres of water in a saucepan over a medium heat and cook the beetroots for 30 minutes, or until soft. Allow to cool. Remove the beetroot skin by rubbing it with your hands (use rubber gloves if you don't want pink-stained fingers) – the skin will slide off easily.

Add the turmeric and tofu cubes to 4 tablespoons of the spiced oil and mix until the tofu is well coated. Pour the remaining spiced oil into a jar with an airtight lid and refrigerate, for later use.

Cut each cooked, cooled beetroot into 8 wedges. In a large mixing bowl combine the beetroot, tofu and spiced oil. Add the spinach and drizzle with balsamic vinegar. Toss gently and serve.

Serves 4

TIP You can keep the leftover spiced oil in an airtight jar in the fridge for up to 4 weeks, and add to all kinds of dishes. Mix it with your favourite vinegar to make a gorgeous salad dressing, or add it to your favourite veggies before roasting.

Chickpea salad with loads of herbs

This delicious salad stays crunchy all day and travels well in a plastic container or jar to work, especially if you keep the dressing separate. It's the herbs that make it so amazing, so make sure you use fresh ones, especially the thyme.

60 ml (¼ cup) olive oil

1 garlic clove, minced

3 tablespoons apple cider vinegar

pinch of salt

tiny pinch of freshly ground black pepper

1 × 400 g can chickpeas, drained

60 g (2 cups) flat-leaf parsley leaves, chopped

1 tablespoon chopped thyme leaves

1 tablespoon chopped oregano leaves

16 basil leaves, chopped

¼ iceberg lettuce, finely sliced

1 orange or yellow capsicum, julienned

To make the dressing, place the olive oil, garlic, vinegar, salt and pepper in a small bowl or jar and stir or shake until well combined. Cover and refrigerate until ready to serve.

In a large bowl, combine all the remaining ingredients and mix well. Cover and refrigerate until ready to serve. Dress the salad just before serving.

Serves 2

TIP If you like to prepare your own pulses, soak ¾ cup dried chickpeas in 750 ml of water overnight. Drain. Place in a saucepan with 1.25 litres of water, bring to the boil and simmer for 1 hour, or until tender.

GLUTEN-FREE

VEGAN

Perfect potato salad

Kipfler potatoes make the perfect potato salad, but new potatoes or small desirees are also excellent. My Viennese grandma inspired this recipe, but I've replaced her generous dollops of rich cream with my favourite shop-bought egg-free mayonnaise.

1 kg kipfler potatoes, scrubbed clean

½ red onion, finely diced

1 large gherkin, diced

2 tablespoons capers, rinsed and chopped

2 tablespoons olive oil

125 ml (½ cup) egg-free mayonnaise

salt and freshly ground black pepper

GLUTEN-FREE

VEGAN

Place the (whole) potatoes in a large saucepan. Add enough water to cover and bring to the boil over a medium heat. Cook at a rolling boil for 15 minutes, or until just tender (test with a skewer). Drain.

While still warm, cut the potatoes into 3 cm chunks.

Place the potatoes in a large serving bowl. Add the remaining ingredients and gently toss together. Serve with Sweet Chilli Barbecue Seitan (page 132) or Sweet and Sticky Tofu (page 116).

Serves 4–6

Avocado toast salad

This is the meal I have when I feel like toast but know I should have salad! Caramelised balsamic vinegar is a more intense, syrupy vinegar, and is easy to find in most large supermarkets and delicatessens. Or you can try making some at home by heating 125 ml of balsamic vinegar in a saucepan over a medium–low heat for 10–20 minutes, or until it has reduced by half.

1 avocado

4 slices of wholegrain bread, toasted

salt and freshly ground black pepper

2 tablespoons olive oil

1 tablespoon caramelised balsamic vinegar

1 tablespoon lemon juice

200 g mixed lettuce leaves

VEGAN

Mash the avocado in a small bowl. Spread the avocado on the toast and sprinkle with salt and pepper. Cut each slice of avocado toast into 9 little squares.

Combine the oil, vinegar and lemon juice in a small jug and mix well.

Place the lettuce in a large salad bowl and drizzle over the dressing. Toss to combine. Add the squares of avocado toast and serve.

Serves 2

Hills hoist bean salad

When I first started making this salad I loved it so much that I ate it almost every day for months! Even now it's still one of my favourites. I used to make this salad at one of the cafes I owned. People would sometimes ask about the meaning of the name and I would have to admit that there wasn't one – I just thought it sounded good! Double the quantities and you'll have a great offering to take to a barbecue.

2 × 400 g cans red kidney beans, drained

60 g (2 cups) flat-leaf parsley leaves, chopped

1 red capsicum, diced

¼ red onion, diced

½ avocado, cubed

½ continental cucumber, diced

3 tablespoons olive oil

2 tablespoons lemon juice

1 garlic clove, minced

salt and freshly ground black pepper

8 large, firm iceberg lettuce leaves, to use as cups

GLUTEN-FREE

VEGAN

In a large mixing bowl, combine all the ingredients except the lettuce. Stir well.

Spoon the bean salad mixture into each lettuce leaf 'cup', and serve 2 per person.

Serves 4

TIP To prepare your own beans, place 1¼ cups of dried kidney beans in a bowl with 800 ml of water and soak overnight. Drain, rinse and place in a saucepan with 1 litre of fresh water. Bring to the boil over a medium heat, reduce the heat and simmer until tender (about 2 hours).

Beer-battered tofu salad

If you don't eat fish and chips but sometimes get a hankering for the crunch of crispy fried batter then you must try this recipe. Yes, it's batter, and yes, it's fried, but it's in a *salad* so it's practically guilt-free! I use rice bran oil for frying as it has a high smoke point. You don't need an electric deep fryer – just use a wok or a deep, heavy-based pan (an enamelled cast-iron pot or stovetop casserole work well).

225 g (1½ cups) self-raising flour

375 ml (1½ cups) beer

1 teaspoon salt

500–750 ml (2–3 cups) rice bran oil for frying

500 g firm tofu, cut into 2 cm cubes

200 g mixed lettuce leaves, washed

250 g cherry tomatoes, halved

salt and freshly ground black pepper

juice of ½ lemon, to serve

VEGAN

To make the batter, place the flour, beer and salt in a large mixing bowl and whisk until smooth.

Heat the oil to 180°C in a wok or a large, heavy-based pan over a high heat. (If you don't have a thermometer, you can tell the oil is ready if it bubbles around the end of a clean wooden spoon when you dip it in.)

Use a fork to dip the tofu pieces into the batter and then drop them in the hot oil. Fry them in batches for 5–7 minutes, or until golden. Drain on paper towel.

Place the lettuce and cherry tomatoes on a serving platter and top with the tofu pieces. Season with salt and pepper and squeeze over the lemon juice. Serve while the tofu is still warm.

Serves 6

My favourite pasta salad

This is a robust, crunchy salad brimming with flavour, colour and texture. It's fabulous as a simple summer dinner or also great to take to work for lunch.

180 g (2 cups) dried penne

2 tablespoons olive oil

3 tablespoons lemon juice

salt and freshly ground black pepper

¼ red cabbage, finely sliced (as fine as you can)

¼ red onion, finely sliced

20 purple grapes

8 semi-dried tomatoes, sliced

2 tablespoons capers, rinsed

100 g (2 cups) flat-leaf parsley leaves, chopped

80 g (½ cup) roasted peanuts

VEGAN

Bring 2 litres of salted water to the boil in a large saucepan or stockpot over a medium–high heat. Add the penne and cook for 11 minutes (or as per packet directions) until al dente. Drain and set aside.

To make the dressing, combine the olive oil and lemon juice in a small bowl or jug. Season with salt and pepper and mix well.

In a large serving bowl, place the cabbage, onion, grapes, semi-dried tomatoes, capers, parsley and peanuts. Pour over the dressing and toss to combine. If you are taking the salad to work, store the dressing and salad in separate airtight containers in the fridge until ready to serve. Consume within 2 days.

Serves 2

TIP A mandoline is a great kitchen tool to help you slice cabbage and other veggies really finely – and quickly!

Kale and fig salad with avocado dressing

Hemp seeds are an amazing source of protein. I used to make this salad with spinach but kale is now so widely available, and takes it to a whole new level. The avocado dressing goes beautifully with any leafy green salad.

375 g (1 bunch) kale, stems removed

juice of ½ lemon

salt

1 tablespoon olive oil

6–8 dried figs, trimmed and chopped

2 tablespoons hemp seeds

50 g (½ cup) pecans, chopped

freshly ground black pepper

AVOCADO DRESSING

½ avocado

3 tablespoons olive oil

2 tablespoons apple cider vinegar

juice of 1 lemon

GLUTEN-FREE

VEGAN

Cut the kale leaves into 2 cm-thick strips. Place in a large serving bowl along with the lemon juice, a pinch of salt and the olive oil. Massage the seasoning through the leaves until they are well coated and softened. Set aside.

To make the dressing, combine the avocado, oil, vinegar and lemon juice in a food processor and blend until smooth.

Pour the dressing over the kale and toss to combine. Add the figs, hemp seeds and pecans and season to taste with salt and freshly ground black pepper. Toss lightly and serve immediately.

Serves 4

Suzy's

Pies, tarts and savoury baking

Sesame and chia biscuits

These crisp little savoury biscuits make an ideal base for appetisers and are great for dips and spreads. I particularly love serving them with guacamole or Spiced Eggplant Dip (page 175).

150 g (1 cup) sesame seeds

1 tablespoon chia seeds

1 tablespoon brown sugar

185 g butter, melted

1 teaspoon vanilla extract

150 g (1 cup) plain flour

½ teaspoon salt

¼ teaspoon baking powder

guacamole (or your favourite dip), to serve

Preheat the oven to 190°C.

Toast the sesame seeds in a small frying pan over a medium–low heat for 10–12 minutes, stirring or shaking them often so they don't burn.

Meanwhile, grind the chia seeds using a mortar and pestle until all the seeds are broken up. Transfer the ground chia seeds to a small jar and add 3 tablespoons of water. Allow to soak for at least 10 minutes.

Combine the brown sugar and melted butter in a large bowl and mix well. Add the vanilla extract, flour, salt, baking powder, toasted sesame seeds and soaked chia seeds and mix thoroughly with a wooden spoon until the mixture is lump-free.

Lightly grease a baking tray.

Drop ½ teaspoonfuls of the mixture onto the baking tray, flatten each one slightly with a spatula. Bake for 10 minutes, or until light brown.

Let the biscuits sit for a couple of minutes to harden up before transferring them to a cooling rack. Once cool, serve with guacamole or any other dip. Store them in an airtight container for up to 2 weeks.

Makes about 20 biscuits

Little tomato and spinach pizzas

As you can probably tell, Italian cuisine is definitely my favourite. When it comes to making pizza, the two most helpful rules to remember are to keep the crust thin and the toppings sparse – less is always more. Vegans can use Notzarella, which is an Australian-made alternative to mozzarella cheese.

BASE

185 g (1¼ cups) plain flour

pinch of salt

1 sachet (7 g) or 1 teaspoon dry yeast

½ teaspoon sugar

1 tablespoon olive oil

120 ml (scant ½ cup) warm water

TOPPING

60 g (¼ cup) tomato puree

50 g (1 cup firmly packed) baby spinach leaves

10 basil leaves, washed

2 tomatoes, sliced

150 g (1 cup) grated mozzarella or Notzarella

freshly ground black pepper

To make the base, sift the flour, salt, yeast and sugar into a large mixing bowl. Make a well in the centre and pour in the olive oil and water. Using a wooden spoon, begin stirring in little circles, gradually incorporating the flour. Keep mixing until you've made a stiff dough. Knead the dough in the bowl to form a ball.

Turn the dough out onto a smooth, clean surface sprinkled with flour and knead for 3 minutes. Return to the mixing bowl, cover and allow to rest in a warm spot for 1 hour, or until the dough has doubled in size.

Preheat the oven to 230°C. Line 2 baking trays with greaseproof paper.

Punch the dough down and turn out onto a smooth, floured surface. Knead for 1 minute. Divide the dough into 10 pieces and roll or press each piece into a small circle about 10 cm in diameter. The bases should be quite thin and the edges slightly thicker (about 1 cm).

Arrange the bases on the baking trays and spread each one with a layer of tomato puree, leaving a 1 cm strip around the perimeter. Lay spinach leaves neatly over the tomato puree. Tear the basil leaves and sprinkle them over the spinach. Add 1–2 slices of tomato to each pizza and sprinkle with mozzarella or Notzarella.

Bake the pizzas for 10–15 minutes, or until the edges are nicely browned. Sprinkle with some freshly ground black pepper. These are delicious hot or cold.

Makes 10 little pizzas

Shepherd's pies

In this recipe I use the perfect replacement for minced meat – textured vegetable protein (TVP). It's made from soybeans and contains the same amount of protein as meat, but without the fat, and you can buy it at almost any health food store.

FILLING

2 tablespoons white miso paste

250 ml (1 cup) hot water

100 g (1 cup) textured vegetable protein (TVP)

2 tablespoons olive oil

1 large onion, diced

2 tomatoes, diced

3 garlic cloves, minced

1 tablespoon tomato paste

salt and freshly ground black pepper

TOPPING

300 g potatoes (about 3 large ones), peeled and cut into chunks

20 g butter

60 ml (¼ cup) milk

¼ teaspoon salt

pinch of freshly ground black pepper

PASTRY

300 g (2 cups) wholemeal flour

pinch of salt

180 g chilled butter, cubed

2 teaspoons sesame oil

60 ml (¼ cup) iced water

To make the pastry, place the flour and salt in a large bowl. Add the butter and sesame oil and rub them into the flour with your fingertips until the mixture resembles breadcrumbs. Add the cold water a few drops at a time until a rough dough forms (you may not need to use all of the water). Sprinkle a clean surface with flour. Turn the dough out onto the surface and knead it 4 or 5 times. Cover in plastic wrap and refrigerate for 30 minutes.

Preheat the oven to 180°C. Grease 8 loose-based tartlet tins (5 cm in diameter) or 8 cups in a 12-cup muffin or tartlet tray.

Place the dough between 2 large sheets of greaseproof paper and roll out to a thickness of about 3 mm with a rolling pin. Use a butter knife to cut circles of pastry 7.5 cm in diameter. Line the tartlet or muffin tins with the pastry circles and place in the fridge for 20 minutes or in the freezer for 10.

Line the pastry shells with greaseproof paper, fill with pastry weights and blind-bake for 10 minutes. Remove from the oven, and carefully remove the paper and weights. Return the shells to the oven for a further 5–7 minutes.

To make the filling, combine the miso paste and hot water in a bowl. Add the TVP and allow it to sit for at least 15 minutes. Heat the oil in a frying pan over a medium heat and sauté the onion until translucent. Add the rehydrated TVP, cover and cook for 5 minutes, stirring once or twice. Add the tomatoes, garlic, tomato paste and 250 ml (1 cup) of water. Reduce the heat to medium–low and cook, covered, for 20 minutes, stirring 3–4 times.

Place the potatoes in a large saucepan of water (enough to cover) and bring to the boil over a medium heat. Cook at a rolling boil for 15 minutes, or until soft (test with a skewer). Drain. Add the butter, milk, salt and pepper. Mash well with a fork or potato masher until smooth.

Spoon the filling into the pastry shells and top with a layer of mashed potato. Bake the pies for 20–30 minutes, or until the edges of the potato are crisp and golden.

Let the pies sit for a few minutes before removing them from the tins.

Makes 8 pies

Tomato, basil and caper flan

Serve this as a lunchtime treat or dress it up with a side of roast vegetables for a stunning dinner dish. If you don't have time to make your own pastry (though this one is super easy as it involves no blind baking), frozen shortcrust or puff pastry will work just as well.

3 tablespoons oil, plus extra for cooking

1 onion, diced

pinch of salt

3 garlic cloves, minced

1 tablespoon capers, rinsed

30 g (1 cup loosely packed) basil leaves

80 g (2 cups loosely packed) baby spinach leaves

3 tomatoes, sliced

PASTRY

360 g (2 cups) wholemeal flour

pinch of salt

165 g chilled dairy-free spread

1 tablespoon lemon juice

2–3 tablespoons iced water

VEGAN

To make the pastry, place the flour and salt in a large bowl. Add the dairy-free spread, rubbing it into the flour with your fingertips until the mixture resembles breadcrumbs. Make a well in the centre and add the lemon juice and 2 tablespoons of the iced water. Mix with a wooden spoon until a dough forms. Add another tablespoon of iced water if the dough is too dry.

Sprinkle a smooth, clean surface with flour. Turn the dough out onto the floured surface and push it together to form a ball. Knead the dough 6–8 times. Wrap in plastic wrap and refrigerate for 20 minutes.

Place the dough between 2 large sheets of greaseproof paper. Use a rolling pin to roll the dough into a large rectangle about 30 x 20 cm. Fold up the edges of the pastry to form a small lip around the perimeter. Use the bottom sheet of greaseproof paper to transfer the pastry to a large baking tray.

Preheat the oven to 190°C.

Heat the oil in small frying pan over a low heat and sauté the onion for 15 minutes. Stir in a pinch of salt. Spoon the onion over the pastry, spreading it out with the back of the spoon. Sprinkle over the garlic, capers and basil leaves. Scatter over the spinach leaves then top with slices of tomato. Drizzle over a little extra oil.

Bake the flan for 15–20 minutes, or until the pastry starts to brown on the edges. Slice and serve hot.

Serves 4

Crispy tofu and spinach pockets

I just love this potato pastry, it's so simple and it crisps up beautifully when baked. These pastry pockets are perfect for lunches on the run or school lunch boxes. The pastry stands up well and the filling remains moist but not soggy.

150 g potatoes (about 2 medium ones), chopped

2 tablespoons olive oil

pinch of salt

170 g (1¼ cups) plain flour

½ teaspoon baking powder

FILLING

2 tablespoons olive oil

1 onion, diced

100 g (2 cups firmly packed) spinach, washed and chopped

1 garlic clove, minced

250 g firm tofu, mashed

1 tablespoon soy sauce

1 teaspoon paprika

VEGAN

Place the potatoes in a small saucepan. Add enough water to cover and bring to the boil over a medium heat. Cook at a rolling boil for 15 minutes, or until soft (test with a skewer). Drain then mash well.

Transfer the potato to a large bowl. Add the olive oil, salt, sifted flour and baking powder and mix until just combined. Make a well in the centre and gradually add 230 ml of cold water, a tablespoon at a time. Mix to form a rough pastry.

Sprinkle a smooth, clean surface with flour. Turn the pastry out onto the floured surface and knead 6–10 times. Wrap in plastic wrap and refrigerate for 20 minutes.

Meanwhile, heat the olive oil in a heavy-based frying pan over a medium heat. Add the onion and sauté for 3–5 minutes, or until translucent. Add the spinach and garlic and sauté for 2–3 minutes, or until the spinach begins to wilt. Add the mashed tofu and sauté for 4–5 minutes. Stir in the soy sauce and paprika and sauté for a further 10 minutes. Remove from the heat and set aside to cool.

Preheat the oven to 180°C. Line a baking tray with greaseproof paper.

Divide the pastry into 4 equal portions. Use a rolling pin to roll out each portion into a circle about 3 mm thick and 20 cm in diameter. Place a quarter of the filling in the centre of each pastry circle. Draw up the sides to make a semi-circular pocket, pinching the pastry edges to seal.

Place the pockets on the tray and bake for 30 minutes, or until the pastry is brown and golden. Serve hot or cold. These would be lovely served with Roasted Brussels Sprouts (page 148), Perfect Potato Salad (page 56) or a simple green salad.

Serves 4

Fresh herb and tofu pie

This pie is a summer favourite. If you want a vegan alternative, you can use dairy-free spread instead of butter, but make sure it's chilled, as this is the secret to creating a crisp, flaky crust.

3 tablespoons rice bran oil

1 large onion, diced

500 g silken tofu

2 teaspoons cornflour

1 large red onion, diced

30 g (1 cup) flat-leaf parsley leaves, chopped

15 g (½ cup) chopped chives

2 tablespoons chopped dill leaves

60 g (¼ cup) olive oil

salt and freshly ground black pepper

PASTRY

360 g (1¾ cups) plain flour

pinch of salt

100 g chilled butter, diced

2–3 tablespoons iced water

To make the pastry, sift the flour and salt into a mixing bowl. Add the butter and rub into the flour with your fingertips until the mixture resembles breadcrumbs. Use a wooden spoon to make a well in the centre. Place 2 tablespoons of the iced water in the well and begin stirring in small circles, gradually incorporating the flour. Keep mixing until you've made a rough dough. If the mixture is not binding well, add the remaining water.

Turn the dough out onto a smooth, clean surface sprinkled with flour. Knead for 2 minutes and shape into a ball. Wrap the dough in plastic wrap and refrigerate for 20 minutes.

Preheat the oven to 190°C. Grease a 25 cm loose-based tart tin.

Place the dough between 2 large sheets of greaseproof paper. Use a rolling pin to roll it out evenly to make a 30 cm circle. Lay the pastry over the tart tin, easing it in to line the base and sides. Trim any overlapping pastry and rest the pastry in the fridge for 20 minutes or the freezer for 10 minutes.

Remove the tin from the fridge and line the pastry shell with greaseproof paper. Fill with baking weights and bake for 15 minutes. Carefully remove the paper and weights and place the pie shell (still in the tin) on a rack to cool.

Reduce the oven to 180°C.

Heat the rice bran oil in a heavy-based frying pan over a medium heat. Add the onion and sauté for 10 minutes, or until soft and golden. Set aside.

Place the tofu and cornflour in a large bowl and mix well. Stir in the sautéed onion, red onion, herbs and olive oil. Season with salt and pepper. Spoon this mixture into the cooled pie shell and bake for 35–40 minutes, or until the filling is firm and brown on top. Serve hot or cold with a salad, such as my Hills Hoist Bean Salad (page 58).

Serves 6

Purple sweet potato and pea pasties

These pasties travel well and are equally tasty hot or cold. Try to make the pastry in advance so that you can whip them up at short notice for a party or when you need to bring a plate. Or simply use store-bought shortcrust or puff pastry. These are vegan, but feel free to substitute the soy and oil with the same quantities of milk and butter.

2 tablespoons rice bran oil

1 white onion, diced

2 garlic cloves, minced

400 g (2 large) purple sweet potato, cut into 1 cm cubes

125 ml (½ cup) coconut milk

salt and freshly ground black pepper

140 g (1 cup) peas (fresh or frozen)

½ head broccoli, chopped

Chunky Tomato Relish (page 176), to serve

PASTRY

125 ml (½ cup) soy milk

2 teaspoons apple cider vinegar

270 g (1½ cups) wholemeal flour

150 g (1 cup) self-raising flour

pinch of salt

1 tablespoon poppy seeds

3 tablespoons olive oil

VEGAN

To make the pastry, pour the soy milk and vinegar into a small bowl. Set aside for 15 minutes, or until bubbles form on the surface. Sift the flours into a large bowl and add the salt and poppy seeds. Use a wooden spoon to make a well in the centre of the flour. Pour in the bubbly soy milk, oil and 125 ml (½ cup) of water. Begin stirring in little circles, gradually incorporating the flour. Keep mixing until you've made a rough dough.

Sprinkle a clean, smooth surface with flour. Turn the dough out onto the floured surface and knead for 3–5 minutes, or until smooth and elastic. Add a drop more water if the dough feels a bit dry, or a sprinkling of flour if it's too moist. Return the dough to the mixing bowl, cover and rest it in a warm spot for 1 hour.

Heat the oil in a heavy-based frying pan over a medium heat and sauté the onion for 3–5 minutes, or until soft and translucent. Add the garlic, sweet potato and coconut milk and season with salt and pepper. Cover and simmer for 10 minutes. Stir in the peas and broccoli, cover and cook for a further 10 minutes, or until the sweet potato is soft. Use a fork to roughly mash all the ingredients together in the pan. Remove pan from the heat and allow to cool.

Preheat the oven to 180°C. Line a large baking tray with greaseproof paper.

Knead the dough again for about 2 minutes on a clean bench and divide into 8 equal pieces. Use a rolling pin to roll out each piece into a circle about 2 mm thick and 15 cm in diameter.

Place 2 tablespoons of filling in the centre of each pastry round. Draw up both sides of the pastry to meet in the centre, pinching the edges to seal. Place the pasties on the baking tray and bake for 40 minutes, or until golden brown. Serve with the tomato relish.

Makes 8 pasties

Mushroom tarts

From the age of 10 I lived on my grandparents' flower farm in Galston in north-west Sydney. They had a huge fruit and veggie garden and grew mushrooms in a rickety old shed. I was fascinated by the bags of sprouting mushrooms and would check on their progress daily. To this day I can still remember the earthy smell of the shed, and making these tarts takes me back there instantly.

15 Swiss brown mushrooms, quartered

150 g oyster mushrooms, halved

4 spring onions, sliced

3 tablespoons olive oil

¼ teaspoon salt

pinch of freshly ground black pepper

2 free-range eggs

80 ml (⅓ cup) milk

1 tablespoon tahini

200 g enoki mushrooms

150 g shelled, unsalted pistachios

PASTRY

300 g (2 cups) plain flour

pinch of salt

180 g chilled butter

1 tablespoon sesame seeds, toasted

1 tablespoon lemon juice

60 ml (¼ cup) iced water

Preheat the oven to 160°C.

Place the Swiss brown and oyster mushrooms in a large casserole dish with a lid. Mix through the spring onions, olive oil, salt and pepper. Cover and bake for 40 minutes until the mushrooms have softened and an amazing aroma hits you when you take off the lid. Allow the mushrooms to cool (keep the lid off).

To make the pastry, place the flour, salt and butter in a large bowl. Rub the butter into the flour with your fingertips until the mixture resembles breadcrumbs. Stir in the sesame seeds and lemon juice. Add the iced water a few drops at a time and mix to form a rough dough (you may not need all the water).

Sprinkle a smooth, clean surface with flour. Turn the dough out onto the floured surface and knead it 5 or 6 times. Cover the dough in plastic wrap and refrigerate for 30 minutes.

Grease 6 loose-based tartlet tins (5 cm wide).

Place the dough between 2 large sheets of greaseproof paper and roll out with a rolling pin to a thickness of 3 mm. Use a butter knife to cut out 6 circles, each 7 cm in diameter. Lay the pastry circles over the tartlet tins, easing the pastry in gently to cover the bases and sides. Place the tins on a baking tray and rest in the fridge for 20 minutes or in the freezer for 10.

Preheat the oven to 180°C.

Line the pastry shells with greaseproof paper. Cover the paper with baking weights and bake for 10 minutes. Carefully remove the paper and weights and return the shells to the oven for 5–7 minutes. Remove from the oven and set aside to cool.

Place the egg, milk and tahini in a small bowl and whisk well. Fill the pastry shells with the baked mushrooms and top with some enoki mushrooms. Pour in about 3 tablespoons of the milk mixture and decorate with pistachios.

Bake the tartlets for 30 minutes, or until firm and golden brown. Serve hot or cold as a starter, or with a leafy green salad as a light lunch.

Makes 6 small tarts

Caramelised onion and tofu tart

This pie looks impressive yet is quite simple. It's also super healthy, with lots of protein, iron, fibre and antioxidants. The lovely, creamy filling is made by blending firm and silken tofu.

PASTRY

360 g (1¾ cups) plain flour

pinch of salt

100 g chilled butter, diced

2–3 tablespoons iced water

CARAMELISED ONIONS

2 onions, sliced

2 tablespoons brown sugar

2 tablespoons balsamic vinegar

pinch of salt

2 tablespoons olive oil

FILLING

250 g firm tofu, rinsed

250 g silken tofu

4 basil leaves, torn into small pieces

2 garlic cloves, minced

2 tablespoons tamari or soy sauce

½ teaspoon salt

¼ teaspoon pepper

200 g (4 cups firmly packed) baby spinach leaves

1 litre (4 cups) boiling water

To make the pastry, sift the flour and salt into a mixing bowl. Add the butter and rub it into the flour with your fingertips until the mixture resembles breadcrumbs. Make a well in the centre. Place 2 tablespoons of the iced water in the well and begin stirring in small circles, gradually incorporating the flour. Keep mixing until you've made a rough dough. If the dough is not binding well, add the remaining water. Turn the dough out onto a smooth, clean surface sprinkled with flour. Gently knead the dough to form a ball. Wrap in plastic wrap and refrigerate for 20 minutes.

Preheat the oven to 190°C. Grease a 25 cm loose-based tart tin.

Remove the dough from the fridge and place it between 2 large sheets of greaseproof paper. Use a rolling pin to roll out into a 30 cm circle. Lay the pastry over the tart tin, easing it in to line the base and sides. Trim any overlapping pastry. Rest the pastry shell in the fridge for 20 minutes or in the freezer for 10.

Remove the pastry shell from the fridge or freezer and line it with greaseproof paper. Fill with baking weights and bake for 15 minutes. Carefully remove the paper and weights and leave the shell (in the tin) to cool on a wire rack.

Reduce the oven to 160°C.

To make the caramelised onions, combine the ingredients in a heavy-based saucepan. Cover and cook over a medium–low heat for 30 minutes, or until the onions are soft and sweet.

Meanwhile, make the filling. Place the firm tofu in a large bowl and use a fork to crumble it. Add the silken tofu and mix well. Mix in the basil, garlic, tamari or soy sauce, salt and pepper.

Place the spinach in a colander over the sink. Pour over the boiling water and press the spinach with a spoon to squeeze out excess water. Add the spinach to the tofu filling and mix well.

Spread the filling evenly on the base of the pastry shell, then top with the caramelised onions. Bake for 1 hour, or until the onions are crispy and the pastry is golden. Serve with a leafy green salad.

Serves 6

Suzy's

Pasta and rice

Pesto and oyster mushroom risotto

The best rice for making risotto is vialone nano, carnaroli or arborio, because they are all brilliant at soaking up flavours and are the creamiest varieties available. But you can actually make a great risotto with any rice, as I learned a couple of years ago when I did the catering on the set of my friend Lester's low-budget film. One day when we were totally broke I used a 4 kg bag of short-grain brown rice I had at home and made a beautiful creamy mushroom risotto. It went down a treat, and we fed 20 hungry people for less than $20!

100 ml olive oil

1 onion, diced

4 garlic cloves, finely chopped

440 g (2 cups) short-grain brown rice, washed

250 ml (1 cup) white wine

900 ml hot water

1 tablespoon salt

250 g oyster mushrooms

freshly ground black pepper

basil leaves

PESTO

3 large handfuls of basil leaves

3 tablespoons olive oil

80 g (½ cup) pine nuts

60 ml (¼ cup) lemon juice

GLUTEN-FREE

VEGAN

Heat 3 tablespoons of the oil in a heavy-based frying pan over a medium heat. Add the onion and sauté for 3–5 minutes, or until translucent. Add the garlic and rice and sauté for 2–3 minutes, stirring gently and constantly to encourage the creamy starch from the rice.

Add the wine and simmer, stirring frequently, for 5 minutes. Stir in the hot water and salt. When the rice begins to simmer, reduce the heat to low. Cook for 20 minutes, covered, stirring frequently. Add an extra ¼ cup of hot water if the rice appears dry or begins to stick to the pan.

In a small frying pan combine the mushrooms with the remaining oil and sauté for 5 minutes. Add a pinch of salt and pepper. Set aside.

To make the pesto, combine all the ingredients in a food processor and process until smooth.

When the rice is cooked, remove from the heat and gently stir through the pesto and mushrooms. Sprinkle with some basil leaves and serve hot.

Serves 6

Naomi's nasi goreng

My friend Naomi made this for me when we were camping up north once. I don't know how she did it because we only had one frying pan! The brown rice gives this dish a heartiness that's perfect after a big day outdoors. Textured vegetable protein is a soy-based minced meat replacement. In this recipe I use a dried variety, but you can also buy it pre-soaked and flavoured in most supermarkets. Fried shallots are available from supermarkets and Asian grocers. Remember to deseed your chillies if you don't like it hot.

440 g (2 cups) brown rice

¼ teaspoon salt

2 tablespoons dark miso paste

100 g (1 cup) textured vegetable protein (TVP)

80 ml (⅓ cup) rice bran oil

1 large white onion, diced

2 small chillies, deseeded and finely chopped

2 teaspoons coriander seeds

6 spring onions cut into 5 cm lengths

4 garlic cloves, finely chopped

3 tablespoons kecap manis (thick sweet Indonesian soy sauce)

80 g (1 cup) bean sprouts

coriander leaves

fried shallots

VEGAN

Combine the rice and salt with 1 litre (4 cups) of water in a heavy-based saucepan and place over a medium heat. Bring to the boil, reduce the heat, cover and cook for 40 minutes, or until the water has evaporated and the rice is soft. Remove the lid and allow the rice to cool (the cooler the better).

Meanwhile, dissolve the miso paste in 250 ml (1 cup) of hot water in a large bowl. Add the textured vegetable protein and leave to soak for at least 15 minutes.

When the TVP is ready, heat the oil in a wok or heavy-based frying pan. Add the onion, chilli and coriander seeds, and cook for 1 minute. Add the re-hydrated TVP and sauté for 1 minute. Add the spring onions, garlic and rice. Sauté for 10 minutes, or until the rice is golden and starts to brown. Stir in the kecap manis and remove from the heat.

Serve hot, garnished with the bean sprouts and coriander leaves and sprinkled with fried shallots.

Serves 4

Rice noodle lasagne

This recipe is inspired by my friend Adam, who is incredibly inventive with rice noodles and wonton wrappers. Traditional lasagne, with its layers of pasta, is usually quite a heavy meal, but the rice noodle sheets in this version give it a lightness that's satisfying without being stodgy.

100 g (2 cups firmly packed) baby spinach leaves

1 litre (4 cups) boiling water

1 kg fresh flat white rice noodle sheets

500 g butternut pumpkin, cut into 5 mm thick slices

salt and freshly ground black pepper

150 g firm tofu, cut into 4 or 5 large thin slices

1 large eggplant, cut into 1 cm-thick slices

TOMATO SAUCE

2 tablespoons olive oil

1 large onion, diced

2 × 400 g cans chopped tomatoes

4 garlic cloves, minced

1 tablespoon tomato paste

5 basil leaves, roughly torn

WHITE SAUCE

60 g dairy-free spread

2 tablespoons cornflour

750 ml (3 cups) soy milk

3 teaspoons savoury yeast flakes

½ teaspoon salt

¼ teaspoon freshly ground black pepper

VEGAN

To make the tomato sauce, heat the olive oil in a saucepan over a medium heat and sauté the onion for 3–5 minutes, or until translucent. Add the tomatoes, garlic, tomato paste and basil leaves. Reduce the heat, cover and simmer for 30 minutes.

Meanwhile, to make the white sauce, melt the dairy-free spread in a saucepan over a medium heat. Stir in the cornflour and cook, stirring constantly, for 2 minutes, or until the flour and dairy-free spread are completely mixed. (This is a 'white roux'.) Slowly add the milk, stirring continuously for 5–10 minutes, or until the sauce thickens. Add the savoury yeast flakes, salt and pepper. Remove from the heat and set aside.

Preheat the oven to 180°C.

Place the spinach in a colander over the sink and carefully pour over the boiling water to wilt it. Drain the spinach well, pressing any excess water out of it and set aside.

Grease the base of a 20 × 30 cm baking dish and line it with a double layer of rice noodle sheets. Cover with a layer of pumpkin slices and ladle over one-third of the tomato sauce, spreading it evenly. Add another double layer of rice noodle sheets, followed by the spinach and a sprinkle of salt and pepper. Ladle another one-third of the tomato sauce over the spinach and cover with another double layer of noodle sheets. Cover with the tofu and spoon over the remaining tomato sauce. Add a final double layer of rice noodle sheets and cover with the eggplant slices. Ladle over the white sauce.

Cover with foil and bake for 40 minutes. Remove the foil and bake for a further 30 minutes, or until nicely brown and crispy on top. This is delicious with a leafy green salad.

Serves 6

Classic stuffed vine leaves

Stuffed vine leaves, or dolmades, are one of my favourite foods of all time. I love the texture of the rice and the sweet and sour flavour of cooked lemon and tomato. They are fun to make and will store for up to 5 days in the fridge.

240 ml (scant 1 cup) olive oil

1 large white onion, finely diced

220 g (1 cup) white short-grain rice

4 garlic cloves, minced

3 tablespoons finely chopped flat-leaf parsley leaves

salt and freshly ground black pepper

30 vine leaves, rinsed and unfolded

juice of 2 lemons

GLUTEN FREE

VEGAN

Preheat the oven to 140°C.

Heat 3 tablespoons of the oil in a saucepan over a medium heat. Add the onion and sauté for 5 minutes, or until translucent. Add the rice and sauté for 4 minutes, stirring frequently, until the rice starts to get creamy. Add 250 ml (1 cup) of water along with the garlic, parsley, salt and pepper. Cover and simmer over a low heat for 10 minutes, or until the water has been absorbed (the rice will still be slightly firm). Set aside.

Place a vine leaf smooth-side down on a clean flat surface. Place a heaped teaspoon of filling into the centre of the vine leaf. Fold the stem end over the filling and then fold over each side, rolling it up to make a little sausage shape. (Don't fold too tightly as the rice will expand a little more during cooking.) Repeat with the remaining rice and vine leaves – you should end up with about 24 dolmades.

Line a heavy-based baking dish with the remaining vine leaves. Snugly pack the rolls seam-side down on the bed of leaves. Pour over the remaining 180 ml (scant ¾ cup) olive oil along with the lemon juice and 500 ml (2 cups) of water. Cover and bake for 1 hour.

Leave in the baking dish with the lid on until cool. Refrigerate before serving.

Serves 6

✻ **TIP** Preserved vine leaves are available from larger supermarkets and most delicatessens and health food stores.

Light and fluffy potato gnocchi

This recipe is guaranteed to produce light and fluffy gnocchi *every* time you make it. Other recipes I've tried have been hit-and-miss, but this one is a beauty. I've served it here with olive oil and rocket, but you can try it with your favourite pasta sauce.

500 g desiree (or other floury) potatoes, peeled

1 teaspoon salt, plus extra to serve

150 g (1 cup) plain flour, plus extra for rolling

olive oil, to serve

2 handfuls of rocket leaves, to serve

freshly ground black pepper

VEGAN

Place the potatoes in a large saucepan. Add enough water to cover and bring to the boil over a medium heat. Cook at a rolling boil for 10 minutes, or until soft (test with a skewer). Drain and cool slightly.

Cut the potatoes into quarters and use the back of a spoon to push them through a sieve (or potato ricer) into a large bowl. Add the salt. Sprinkle a quarter of the flour over the potato and work it in with your fingers. Add the rest of the flour, a bit at a time. Knead in the bowl to form a rough dough, adding a little more flour if it feels too sticky.

Sprinkle a clean, smooth surface with flour. Place the dough in the centre of the flour, and knead for 1–2 minutes until smooth and velvety.

Divide the dough into 3 pieces. Roll each piece into a 2 cm-thick sausage then cut each length into 1 cm pieces. Roll each piece into a little oval shape. Place the oval on a fork and gently flatten with your index finger (this ensures they cook evenly and also gives the olive oil somewhere to cling). Repeat with the remaining dough.

Bring 2 litres of salted water to the boil in a large saucepan or stockpot over a medium–high heat. Drop the gnocchi into the boiling water and simmer for 2–3 minutes, or until the gnocchi rise to the top. Scoop out with a slotted spoon and transfer to a warmed serving bowl.

Drizzle with a little olive oil, scatter over the rocket leaves and season with salt and pepper. Serve immediately.

Serves 2

Spaghetti bolognese

Quite a few people have told me that they'd love to be vegetarian but that they just couldn't live without spaghetti bolognese. Whenever they do, I give them this recipe. We make it about once a week at home – you could say it's a Spoon family staple. This version is vegan, but vegetarians might like to serve it with some freshly grated parmesan.

2 tablespoons dark miso paste

500 ml (2 cups) hot water

200 g (2 cups) textured vegetable protein (TVP)

60 ml (¼ cup) olive oil

1 large onion, diced

¼ teaspoon dried oregano

¼ teaspoon dried basil

4 garlic cloves, minced

pinch of salt

8 tomatoes, diced

3 tablespoons tomato paste

350 g dried spaghetti

small handful of basil leaves

VEGAN

Combine the miso paste and hot water in a large bowl. Add the TVP and mix well. Set aside to soak for 15 minutes.

Heat the olive oil in a large frying pan over a medium heat. Add the onion and sauté for 3–5 minutes, or until translucent. Add the oregano, basil, garlic, salt and TVP and cook for 10 minutes. Add the tomatoes, tomato paste and 375 ml (1½ cups) of water. Simmer for 45 minutes, stirring regularly, until the sauce is nice and thick.

Meanwhile, bring 2 litres of salted water to the boil in a large saucepan or stockpot over a medium–high heat. Add the spaghetti and cook for 9 minutes (or as per packet directions) until al dente. Drain, reserving 2 tablespoons of the cooking liquid.

Add the reserved cooking liquid to the sauce and stir. Divide the pasta between serving bowls and top with the steaming bolognese. Garnish with fresh basil leaves.

Serves 6

Simple but tasty chilli pasta

This is a great lunch, especially if you're doing physical work. It's quick and easy to make, and after lunch you can power on, burning off all those carbs. It's nice cold, too, so you can take it on a bushwalk or kayaking or wherever you need to go.

150 g dried fusilli (spiral pasta)

3 tablespoons olive oil

¼ teaspoon salt

1 large white onion, finely diced

2 slices of stale vegan bread, very finely diced

½ long red chilli, finely sliced

1 small red chilli, finely sliced

4 garlic cloves, finely chopped

2 tablespoons balsamic vinegar

2 tablespoons capers, rinsed

salt and freshly ground black pepper

finely chopped flat-leaf parsley leaves

VEGAN

Bring 2 litres of salted water to the boil in a large saucepan or stockpot over a high heat. Add the pasta and cook for 11 minutes (or as per packet directions) until al dente. Drain, reserving 2 tablespoons of the cooking liquid. Return the pasta to the pot, drizzle over 2 tablespoons of the oil and sprinkle with salt flakes. Cover and keep warm. Set aside.

Heat the remaining oil in a frying pan over a medium heat. Add the onion and sauté for 3–5 minutes, or until soft and translucent. Add the bread, chilli and garlic and sauté for 10 minutes. Stir in the vinegar and capers.

Combine the pasta and onion mix in a large serving bowl. Add the reserved cooking liquid and stir through gently. Season with salt and pepper, sprinkle over some parsley and serve immediately.

Serves 4

Suzy's

Legumes, lentils and grains

Mung bean, brown rice and zucchini balls

This is a great recipe for parents who have to play 'hide the vegetables' with their children. My nieces and nephews eat these as quickly as I can make them and nobody seems to notice that they are full of zucchini, too.

100 g (½ cup) mung beans

110 g (1½ cups) brown rice

1 onion, diced

¼ loaf day-old bread, finely diced

1 zucchini, grated

2 tablespoons chopped dill leaves

4 garlic cloves, minced

2 tablespoons olive oil

100 g (1 cup) breadcrumbs

3 tablespoons sesame seeds, toasted

500 ml (2 cups) oil

salt and freshly ground black pepper

grated lime zest

Sesame and Lime Dressing (page 172), to serve

VEGAN

Place the mung beans in a sieve and rinse well under running water. Drain and transfer to a saucepan with 500 ml (2 cups) of water. Bring to the boil over a medium heat and simmer, uncovered, for 40 minutes, or until soft. Drain and set aside.

Meanwhile, place the rice in a sieve and rinse well under running water. Drain and transfer to another saucepan with 375 ml (1½ cups) of water. Cover and bring to the boil over a medium heat. Reduce the heat and simmer for 15–20 minutes, or until fluffy.

In a large bowl combine the beans, rice, onion and bread. Mix well.

Place the grated zucchini in a clean tea towel and press gently to remove excess liquid. Add the zucchini to the bean and rice mixture along with the dill, garlic, olive oil and breadcrumbs. Mix until nice and sticky.

Place the sesame seeds in a small bowl. With clean, wet hands shape the bean mixture into little balls. Roll the balls in the sesame seeds and coat evenly.

Heat the oil in a frying pan over a medium heat. Cook the balls in batches (depending on the size of your pan) for about 10–15 minutes, turning regularly, until they are golden brown and crisp all over. Drain on paper towel.

Transfer to a serving plate and sprinkle with salt, pepper and a little grated lime zest. Serve hot with the sesame and lime dressing for dipping.

Serves 4

TIP To toast the sesame seeds, heat a small frying pan over a medium heat. Add the seeds and toast for about 10 minutes, stirring often to prevent burning.

Pearl barley and pinto bean stew

This wholesome and hearty soup is a good reminder that delicious food doesn't need to be fancy. I love having a pot of this simmering on the stove when everyone gets home, especially in winter. Barley is a bit of a forgotten grain, but has a great, nutty flavour and is high in fibre, minerals and protein. 'Pearl' just means the outer husk has been removed, and the bran polished away.

60 ml (¼ cup) olive oil

1 small onion, diced

2 carrots, cut into chunks

2 celery sticks, chopped

1 parsnip, cut into chunks

½ teaspoon salt

¼ teaspoon freshly ground black pepper

4 garlic cloves, finely chopped

200 g (1 cup) pearl barley

2 tablespoons white miso paste

1 × 250 g can pinto beans, drained

6 slices of sourdough bread

1 garlic clove, peeled and halved

olive oil

Heat the oil in a large heavy-based saucepan over a medium heat. Add the onion, carrot, celery, parsnip, salt and pepper and sauté for 10 minutes. Stir in the garlic. Add the barley, miso paste and 1.6 litres of water. Simmer for 30 minutes, or until the barley is plump and soft. Add the pinto beans and simmer for 10 minutes.

Toast the sourdough bread and rub each slice with the cut side of the garlic. Brush with a little olive oil.

Ladle the soup into bowls and serve with the garlic toast.

Serves 6

TIP If you prefer to use dried pintos, soak 1 cup of beans in 750 ml of water overnight. Drain, rinse and place in a saucepan with 1 litre of fresh water. Bring to the boil over a medium heat. Reduce the heat and simmer for 2 hours, or until tender. Add salt to taste just before the beans are ready. Drain.

VEGAN

Sunday nut roast

When I serve this superb nut roast for Christmas dinner, even the meatasauruses adore it. We try to have it as often as we can, and when we do it's a feast and everybody's welcome.

250 g (about 3) potatoes, peeled and quartered

3 tablespoons olive oil, plus extra for roasting

¼ loaf of vegan bread, diced

2 tablespoons finely chopped sage leaves

2 tablespoons finely chopped thyme leaves

3 tablespoons finely chopped rosemary leaves

50 g (1 cup tightly packed) flat-leaf parsley leaves, chopped

3 garlic cloves, minced

2 x 400 g cans of lima beans

3 tablespoons Caramelised Onion (page 83)

150 g unsalted cashew nuts, roughly chopped

150 g almonds, roughly chopped

150 g unsalted shelled pistachios

VEGAN

Place the potatoes in a small saucepan, cover with water and bring to the boil over a medium heat. Cook at a rolling boil for 15 minutes, or until soft (test with a skewer). Drain and set aside.

Heat the oil in a frying pan over a medium heat. Add the bread cubes and stir until well-coated. Add the sage, thyme and 2 tablespoons of the rosemary and sauté the bread and herbs for 4 minutes until aromatic. Transfer the bread to a large bowl along with the parsley, garlic, beans and caramelised onion.

Mash the potato in the pot using a fork (it should be a little bit lumpy). Transfer the potato to the bread mixture along with the nuts and mix thoroughly. (This mixture should be soft with crunchy bits through it, but firm enough to mould into a shape.)

Tip the mixture out onto a clean surface and use your hands to form a loaf shape about 25 cm long and 12 cm wide. Place a clean tea towel or 60 x 40 cm piece of cheesecloth next to the loaf. Place the loaf at the short end of the cloth, folding over the excess fabric on each side. Now roll it up in the cloth and secure it by tying string around the loaf in 3 or 4 places.

Bring 3 litres of water to boil in a large stockpot over a high heat. Place the loaf into a steamer or colander and lower it over the boiling water. Cover, and steam the loaf for 1 hour.

Preheat the oven to 180°C. Grease a large baking tray.

Remove the loaf from the steamer and let it cool for 10 minutes. Cut the string and remove the cheesecloth or tea towel. Place the loaf on the baking tray. Brush the top and sides with olive oil and sprinkle over the remaining rosemary. Roast for 45 minutes, or until crisp and golden brown. Serve with your favourite roast vegetables and gravy.

Serves 8

Lentil and pine nut patties

These patties are very high in protein and dietary fibre and make a perfect portable lunch. They are especially delicious in a sandwich with mayonnaise and snow pea sprouts. I use sunflower oil in this recipe but you can use rice bran oil, canola oil or olive oil.

1 large potato (about 100 g), skin on and cut into quarters

3 tablespoons pine nuts

½ large onion, very finely diced

2 x 400 g cans of brown lentils

3 garlic cloves, minced

100 g (1 cup) breadcrumbs

50 g (½ cup) almond meal

salt and freshly ground black pepper

60 ml (¼ cup) sunflower oil

VEGAN

Place the potato in a small saucepan of water (enough to cover) and bring to the boil over a medium heat. Cook at a rolling boil for 10 minutes, or until soft (test with a skewer). Drain and leave to cool.

Meanwhile, heat a small frying pan over a medium heat. Pop in the pine nuts and gently toast them for 3–5 minutes until they are golden all over. Shake or stir them regularly so they don't burn. Set aside.

Transfer the potato to a large mixing bowl and mash roughly using a fork or potato masher. Add the onion, lentils, garlic, breadcrumbs, pine nuts, almond meal and season to taste with salt and pepper. Mix thoroughly. Shape the mixture into small patties using clean, wet hands.

Heat the oil in large heavy-based frying pan over a medium heat. Cook the patties on both sides for 3–5 minutes, or until browned and crunchy. Serve hot in a toasted bun with lettuce, sliced tomato and mayo, or have one cold with your favourite salad.

Serves 4

TIP To prepare your own lentils, wash 1 cup of dried lentils in a sieve. Drain. Transfer to a saucepan with 750 ml of fresh water and bring to the boil over a medium heat. Reduce the heat and simmer, uncovered, for 30–40 minutes until lentils are just tender.

Sage and garlic bean burgers

This is a superb burger recipe because the patty gets crispy on the outside while remaining moist on the inside. Great northern beans are a firm, white, Australian-grown bean that you should be able to find in any large supermarket, health food store or deli. If you can't, butter beans or cannellini beans work just as well.

1 large desiree potato (about 100 g), peeled

1 × 400 g can great northern beans, drained

1 small onion, finely diced

4 garlic cloves, minced

100 g (1 cup) breadcrumbs

4 tablespoons chopped sage leaves, plus 8 whole sage leaves

1 teaspoon salt

60 ml (¼ cup) olive oil

sliced bread or buns, to serve

baby spinach leaves, to serve

MacDonna's Vegan Mayo or Chunky Tomato Relish (pages 168 and 176), to serve

VEGAN

Place the potato in a small saucepan of water (enough to cover) and bring to the boil over a medium heat. Cook at a rolling boil for about 15 minutes, or until soft (test with a skewer). Drain.

Place the potato in a large mixing bowl and mash well. Add the beans, onion, garlic, breadcrumbs, chopped sage and salt and use your hands to 'massage' the mixture until it is nice and sticky.

Wash your hands and keep them wet to more easily shape the mixture into 8 firm patties. Decorate one side of each patty with a whole sage leaf, pressing it in slightly to make sure it sticks.

Heat the oil in a large heavy-based frying pan or on a barbecue hotplate. Cook the patties for 3 minutes on each side, or until crispy and browned.

Serve on slices of bread or buns with baby spinach and a generous dollop of mayo or relish. Or enjoy them with a big salad or some steamed vegetables.

Makes 8 burgers

TIP If you prefer to prepare your own pulses, soak 1 cup of dried great northern beans in 750 ml of water overnight. Drain. Transfer to a saucepan with 1.25 litres of fresh water and bring to the boil over a medium heat. Boil, uncovered, for 60–80 minutes, or until tender.

Very moreish mung bean cakes

Not many people cook with dried mung beans, perhaps because they have a bit of a 'hippy food' stigma. If you've never tried mung beans, this recipe is a scrumptious introduction. These cakes make great party food, but you could also serve them with Spiced Tofu and Beetroot Salad (page 52) for a wholesome lunch.

200 g (1 cup) dried mung beans

150 g (1 cup) plain flour

5 spring onions, sliced

2 garlic cloves, finely chopped

2 small chillies, deseeded and finely chopped

1 tablespoon sugar

125 ml (½ cup) rice bran oil

1 teaspoon salt

Hot Chilli Jam (page 166), to serve

VEGAN

Place the mung beans in a bowl with 1 litre (4 cups) of water and set aside to soak for 1 hour.

Drain the beans and transfer them to a large, heavy-based saucepan with 875 ml (3½ cups) of water. Place over a low heat, cover and cook for 35 minutes, or until the beans have absorbed all the water.

Meanwhile, combine 75 g (½ cup) of the flour with 150 ml of water in a jug or bowl. Use a wooden spoon to stir the mixture to form a smooth batter. Set aside while you prepare the other ingredients.

Transfer the mung beans to a large bowl. Add the spring onions (reserving a few to garnish), garlic, chilli, sugar and remaining flour and mix well.

Heat the oil in heavy-based frying pan over a medium–high heat. Shape the bean mixture into golf-ball-sized balls then flatten them slightly between your hands. Use a fork to dip the balls in the batter and then pop them in the pan, a few at a time. Fry for 3 minutes on each side, or until golden and crunchy. Drain on paper towel. Repeat until all the mixture is used up.

Sprinkle with the salt and reserved spring onion and serve immediately with chilli jam.

Serves 4

Green beans with lentils and dill

This amazing little dish was a popular staff choice at the Surry Hills cafe I worked in many years ago. It's so quick to prepare yet is bursting with flavour. I love that the beans stay bright green and crunchy and the lentils are soft and earthy. It's still one of my favourites! Use small lentils (such as Italian, black beluga or small green French or Puy lentils).

300 g fresh green beans, trimmed

700 ml iced water

40 g (¼ cup) pine nuts

3 tablespoons olive oil

½ red onion, diced

½ garlic clove, finely chopped

1 × 400 g can of small lentils, drained and rinsed

1 tablespoon golden syrup

2 teaspoons seeded mustard

1 tablespoon apple cider vinegar

pinch each of salt and freshly ground black pepper

3 tablespoons finely chopped dill leaves

1 tablespoon chopped mint leaves

Half fill a saucepan with water and bring it to the boil over a medium heat. Place the beans in a steamer or metal colander over the boiling water and steam for 4–5 minutes. Drain.

Plunge the beans in a bowl with the iced water. Drain and set aside.

Heat a heavy-based frying pan over a medium heat. Add the pine nuts and keep them moving in the pan for 1–2 minutes, or until they begin to take on colour. Add the oil, onion and garlic and sauté for 1 minute. Add the lentils, green beans, golden syrup, mustard and vinegar. Cook for 3–5 minutes, or until the lentils and beans are heated through.

Remove from the heat and gently stir through the salt, pepper, dill and mint. Serve immediately.

Serves 2–3

TIP To prepare your own lentils, wash ¾ cup of dried small green French lentils in a sieve. Drain. Transfer to a saucepan with 750 ml of fresh water and bring to the boil over a medium heat. Reduce the heat and simmer, uncovered, for 30–40 minutes until lentils are just tender.

GLUTEN-FREE

VEGAN

Buckwheat and black bean cakes

The fresh coriander, lime and garlic in this dish are the perfect complement to the nutty, earthy flavours of the buckwheat and beans. You will need a ring mould (8 cm diameter x 6 cm tall) and a mortar and pestle or food processor for this recipe. You can find cans of black turtle beans in health food stores.

200 g (1 cup) buckwheat

2 tablespoons ground flax seeds

100 g (½ cup) canned black turtle beans

1 red onion, finely diced

1 teaspoon lime zest

3 tablespoons plain flour

2 tablespoons savoury yeast flakes

2 teaspoons ground coriander

1 teaspoon salt

pinch of freshly ground black pepper

100 ml olive oil

½ garlic clove

1 large handful of coriander leaves

juice of 1 lime

VEGAN

Place the buckwheat in a small saucepan with 500 ml (2 cups) of water. Bring to the boil over a medium heat. Reduce the heat, cover and simmer gently for 30 minutes, or until the water has been absorbed and the buckwheat is tender.

Meanwhile, combine the flax seeds with 3 tablespoons of water in a small bowl or cup. Set aside for 15 minutes until the mixture becomes a thick gel.

Place the buckwheat and black beans in a large bowl with the onion, lime zest and flax gel. Mix well with a wooden spoon. Stir in the flour, yeast flakes, ground coriander, salt and pepper.

Grease a ring mould and place the mould on a plate. Spoon the buckwheat mixture into the mould, pressing it until it is filled to the top. Carefully remove the mould to leave behind a little buckwheat 'cake'. Repeat with the remaining mixture until you have 6 buckwheat cakes.

Heat 2 tablespoons of the oil in a heavy-based frying pan. Add the buckwheat cakes and cook for about 7 minutes on each side, or until browned.

Meanwhile, use a large mortar and pestle to grind the garlic and fresh coriander (stalks and all) into a paste. Add the lime juice and the remaining 3 tablespoons of the olive oil and grind again to lubricate the paste. (Alternatively, you can put all the ingredients in a food processor and process to a smooth paste.)

To serve, dollop spoonfuls of the coriander paste on a platter, then top with the buckwheat cakes.

Serves 2–4

Seitan, tofu and tempeh

Sweet and sticky tofu

If you'd like to replicate the sweet, sticky sensation of barbecued ribs without the ribs then this recipe is for you. For best results, marinate the tofu for at least 2 hours (preferably overnight). If you're okay with gluten, you can use seitan instead of the tofu, to get that extra-chewy texture. These are delicious with Barbecued Field Mushrooms (page 146) and Flame-cooked Chilli Corn (page 151).

250 g firm tofu

3 tablespoons tamari

50 g (¼ cup) brown sugar

3 tablespoons rice malt syrup

½ tablespoon finely grated ginger

2 garlic cloves, minced

1 tablespoon chilli flakes

3 tablespoons olive oil, plus extra for frying

GLUTEN-FREE

Cut the tofu into 1 cm-thick finger lengths and dry them on paper towel. Lay the tofu slices in a shallow dish.

Place the remaining ingredients in a small bowl and mix well. Spoon the mixture over the tofu, cover and marinate for at least 2 hours (overnight if possible) in the fridge.

Heat a drop of oil in a frying pan or on a barbecue plate over a medium heat and sear the tofu for 3–4 minutes each side, or until brown and sticky. Serve hot, with your favourite dipping sauce, a salad or veggie side of your choice.

Serves 2

Tuscan tofu balls in tomato sauce

This vegetarian version of the classic Italian dish is a beauty. The walnuts give the tofu balls a full-bodied flavour and texture that is perfect with the rich tomato and basil sauce. Bellissimo!

3 tablespoons olive oil

½ onion, diced

1 × 400 g can of diced tomatoes

1 garlic clove, minced

1 teaspoon sugar

225 g dried spaghetti

freshly grated parmesan, to serve

TOFU BALLS

280 g firm tofu, crumbled

40 g (⅓ cup) walnuts, finely chopped

½ onion, finely diced

1 garlic clove, minced

20 g (¼ cup) breadcrumbs

2 tablespoons chopped basil leaves

2 tablespoons olive oil

Heat the oil in a heavy-based frying pan over a medium heat. Add the onion and sauté for 3–5 minutes, or until translucent. Add the tomatoes, garlic, sugar and 250 ml (1 cup) of water and simmer for 30 minutes.

While the spaghetti is cooking, make the tofu balls. Place the tofu and walnuts in a large bowl and give them a good mix. Add the onion, garlic, breadcrumbs and fresh basil. Use your hands (clean of course!) to massage the mixture for 2–3 minutes until it is well combined and sticky. Wash your hands, wet them, and roll tablespoonfuls of the tofu mixture into little balls about 3 cm in diameter. Set aside.

Heat 2 litres of water in a large saucepan over a medium heat. When bubbling, add the spaghetti and cook for 11 minutes (or as per packet instructions) until al dente. Remove from the heat, drain, return to the pot and cover.

While the spaghetti is cooking, finish preparing the tofu balls. Heat the oil in a heavy-based frying pan over a medium heat. Cook the balls for 7–10 minutes, rolling them around so they brown evenly.

Serve the balls on a bed of spaghetti topped with the tomato sauce and freshly grated parmesan.

Serves 4

Golden tempeh fingers

Tempeh is made from fermented soybeans. Its lovely, nutty flavour and firm texture make it very versatile for cooking, and it also happens to be highly nutritious (it contains plenty of protein and lots of B vitamins). These golden tempeh fingers are mouth-wateringly delicious as a snack served with lemon and coriander dipping sauce, but you could also cut them up and add them to a leafy salad.

100 g (1 cup) breadcrumbs

1 tablespoon sesame seeds

1 tablespoon dried garlic powder

1 tablespoon savoury yeast flakes

½ teaspoon ground black pepper

pinch of ground white pepper

½ teaspoon salt

½ teaspoon ground chilli

150 g (1 cup) plain flour

500 ml (2 cups) milk

500 g tempeh, sliced into 1 cm thin strips

60 ml (¼ cup) rice bran oil for frying

Lemon and Coriander Dipping Sauce (page 172), to serve

VEGAN

To make the coating, combine the breadcrumbs, sesame seeds, garlic powder, yeast flakes, black and white pepper, salt, chilli and onion flakes in a large bowl and mix well. Set aside.

Spoon the plain flour into a strong, clean plastic bag. Pour the milk into a large bowl.

Place the tempeh strips in the flour bag and shake gently until well coated. Remove strips from the bag and dust off the excess flour. Use a fork to dunk each strip in the milk then roll it in the spiced crumbs. Repeat the process until all the tempeh strips are crumbed.

Heat the oil in a large wok or heavy-based pan over a medium–high heat. Fry the tempeh for 2–4 minutes on each side, or until golden brown. Drain on paper towel. Serve hot with the dipping sauce.

Serves 4

Hard mud burger with peanut sauce

This might not sound delicious, but believe me, it is! If you're not up to making your own mayo, just use your favourite store-bought variety.

2 tablespoons olive oil

1 large onion, sliced

½ teaspoon brown sugar

½ teaspoon balsamic vinegar

2 tablespoons crunchy natural peanut butter

2 tablespoons sweet chilli sauce

2 × 1 cm-thick slices of tempeh

2 bread rolls

2 tablespoons MacDonnas' Vegan Mayo (see page 168)

1 tomato, sliced

2 large lettuce leaves

VEGAN

Heat 1 tablespoon of the oil in a saucepan over a medium–low heat. Add the onion, sugar and vinegar and cook for 10–15 minutes, or until the onion caramelises and its edges start to crisp up. Set aside and keep warm.

In a small bowl combine the peanut butter and chilli sauce with 3 tablespoons of water and mix well with a fork until smooth and glossy. Set aside.

Heat the remaining oil in a heavy-based frying pan over a medium heat. Cook the tempeh for 3–4 minutes on each side, or until golden. Be careful not to burn the tempeh – it will taste better slightly underdone than overdone. Set aside and keep warm.

Cut the rolls in half and lightly toast the insides under a grill. Transfer immediately to serving plates and spread each bun with mayo. Place the tempeh on the bottom half and spoon over the onion and a generous dollop of peanut sauce. Add tomato, lettuce and the top of the bun and there you go. So simple yet so delicious!

Serves 2

Pan-fried chilli tempeh

When you're short on time, this recipe is a beauty. It works equally well with tofu, but I prefer the lovely, nutty flavour of tempeh.

1 tablespoon plain flour

1 tablespoon savoury yeast flakes

250 g tempeh, cut into 4 x 1 cm-thick slices

2 long red chillies, deseeded and finely sliced lengthways

1 spring onion, sliced finely into finger-length strips

3 tablespoons rice bran oil

rice and steamed vegetables, to serve

VEGAN

Place the flour and yeast flakes in a small mixing bowl. Add 150 ml of water and whisk to make a thin, smooth batter.

Use a fork to dip the slices of tempeh into the batter one at a time and lay them on a plate. Decorate the tempeh with the chilli and spring onion.

Heat the oil in a heavy-based frying pan over medium–high heat. Add the tempeh and cook for 5 minutes on each side, or until golden brown and crispy. Take care when flipping the tempeh to keep the chilli and spring onion in place.

Serve hot with rice and steamed vegetables, or your favourite salad.

Serves 2

Smoky tempeh sandwich

This is no ordinary sandwich – I've created a spicy marinade for the tempeh using a dash of liquid smoke, which (you guessed it) imparts a rich, smoky flavour.

320 g tempeh, sliced lengthways as thinly as possible

2 tablespoons olive oil

sea salt flakes and freshly ground black pepper

8 slices of bread

2 tablespoons mayonnaise

100 g (½ punnet) snow pea sprouts

MARINADE

2 tablespoons golden syrup

2 tablespoons olive oil

1 teaspoon ground cumin

tiny pinch of cayenne pepper

1 teaspoon paprika

1 teaspoon liquid smoke

1 garlic clove, minced

1 teaspoon soy sauce

Place all the marinade ingredients in a dish and mix well. Lay the tempeh slices in the marinade, making sure they are well-coated, and set aside for 15 minutes.

Heat the olive oil in a frying pan over a medium–high heat. Lay the tempeh slices flat in the frying pan and cook for 1 minute on each side, or until browned and crispy. Drain on paper towel. Season with salt and pepper.

Spread each slice of bread with mayonnaise then assemble your sandwiches starting with a layer of tempeh and topping it with the sprouts. Cut each sandwich in half and serve.

Serves 4

Chilli and coconut seitan

These seitan pieces have a great texture and are delicious in wraps or salads. If you don't have time to make my hot chilli jam for the marinade, a shop-bought chilli jam will be fine. Make sure you use toasted sesame oil (look for it in the Asian food section of your supermarket) – it's darker and has a stronger flavour and aroma than untoasted sesame oil.

2 tablespoons dark miso paste

2 garlic cloves, minced

1 tablespoon toasted sesame oil

2 tablespoons savoury yeast flakes

½ teaspoon ground nutmeg

½ teaspoon cinnamon

185 g (1¼ cups) wheat gluten flour

3 tablespoons soy sauce

3 garlic cloves, smashed

1 bay leaf

MARINADE

4 garlic cloves, minced

3 tablespoons Hot Chilli Jam (page 166)

1 teaspoon ground allspice

1 teaspoon ground cardamom

½ teaspoon whole cloves

½ teaspoon ground nutmeg

250 ml (1 cup) coconut cream

juice of ½ lemon

2 tablespoons olive oil

salt and freshly ground black pepper

To make the seitan, dissolve the miso paste in 250 ml (1 cup) of water in a large mixing bowl. Stir in the garlic, sesame oil, savoury yeast flakes, nutmeg and cinnamon. Fold in the gluten flour and mix with a wooden spoon until a springy and resistant dough forms. Knead the dough in the bowl for 3 minutes, alternately pressing it down with the heel of your hand and folding it over. Set the dough aside to rest for 10 minutes.

Divide the dough into 3 equal pieces. Place the first piece between 2 sheets of greaseproof paper and roll out with a rolling pin to a thickness of 3–4 cm. It will be quite springy and resist your efforts to shape it, but be persistent. Repeat with the remaining dough pieces.

In a large saucepan or stockpot bring 2 litres of water to the boil over a medium heat. Add the soy sauce, garlic, bay leaf and seitan. Reduce the heat and simmer very gently for 2 hours (seitan will puff up if it is cooked too quickly). Add more water if needed. Remove the seitan with a slotted spoon and drain on paper towel. Transfer the seitan to a cutting board and slice into long thin strips.

Combine all the marinade ingredients in a large bowl and mix well. Add the seitan strips and stir well to ensure they are covered in marinade. Cover and refrigerate overnight.

When you are ready to cook the seitan, heat a barbecue grill plate or frying pan over a medium heat and fry for 3–5 minutes on each side, or until nicely browned.

Serve with rice or a salad. This goes beautifully my Kale and Fig Salad with Avocado Dressing (page 65).

Serves 4

VEGAN

Seitan and veggie skewers

I love to rock up to a barbecue with a platter of such beautiful-looking vegetarian food that even the carnivores are curious. These seitan skewers are just the ticket. You can add any fresh vegetables you have and even marinate them if you have time. It's a good idea to make these the day before you need them as the seitan needs to cook for 2 hours.

2 tablespoons dark miso paste

2 garlic cloves, minced

1 tablespoon toasted sesame oil

2 tablespoons savoury yeast flakes

185 g (1¼ cups) wheat gluten flour

60 ml (¼ cup) soy sauce

3 garlic cloves, smashed

1 bay leaf

1 red capsicum, cut into 3 cm chunks

1 yellow capsicum, cut into 3 cm chunks

250 g (1 punnet) cherry tomatoes

1 red onion, cut into chunks

300 g button mushrooms

2 tablespoons olive oil

salt and freshly ground black pepper

Chunky Tomato Relish (page 176), to serve

VEGAN

Soak 18 wooden skewers in water (this prevents them from burning during cooking).

Dissolve the miso paste in 250 ml (1 cup) of water in a large bowl. Stir in the garlic, sesame oil, savoury yeast flakes and flour. Mix with a wooden spoon until a springy and resistant dough forms. Knead in the bowl for 3 minutes, pushing it away gently and rolling back. Set aside to rest for 10 minutes. Divide into 3 equal pieces.

Bring 2 litres of water to the boil in a large saucepan or stockpot over a medium heat. Add the soy sauce, smashed garlic, bay leaf and dough pieces. Reduce the heat to low and simmer gently, covered, for 2 hours (the seitan will puff up if cooked too quickly; we want it dense and heavy rather than spongy). Add more boiled water if needed.

Remove the seitan with a slotted spoon and drain on paper towel. Allow it to cool. (The pieces will have increased in size and should be quite firm.)

Cut the seitan into 4–5 cm chunks. Thread a piece of seitan onto a skewer, followed by a piece each of capsicum, onion, tomato and mushroom. Repeat until the skewer is full, leaving a bare section at the bottom for holding onto. Repeat the process with the remaining skewers until you have used all the ingredients. Drizzle the kebabs with the olive oil, and season with salt and pepper. Cover and refrigerate until ready to cook.

Heat a char-grill pan or barbecue hotplate over a medium heat. Cook the kebabs, turning regularly, for 10 minutes, or until they are browned on all sides. Serve hot with tomato relish. These are also great with my Hills Hoist Bean Salad (page 58) or a simple leafy green salad.

Serves 4

Kanaga's 'not chicken' curry

Vegetarians and vegans have some great options when it comes to meat alternatives and these are most often made with plant proteins from wheat or soy. Asian grocery stores often sell a great selection of 'not meat' products and one of my favourites is nuggets made from seitan or soy. My dear friend Kanaga makes this amazing Sri Lankan 'not chicken' curry with these nuggets, and is happy for me to share his recipe with you.

3 tablespoons olive oil

1 teaspoon yellow mustard seeds

1½ large onions, diced

6 garlic cloves, finely chopped

3 tablespoons finely chopped ginger

10 fresh curry leaves

1 teaspoon ground cumin

½ teaspoon fennel seeds

1 teaspoon dill seeds

1 tablespoon chilli powder

500 g seitan/soy nuggets

2 tomatoes, diced

¾ teaspoon salt

125 ml (½ cup) coconut milk

steamed rice, to serve

1 long red chilli, halved, deseeded and sliced

VEGAN

Heat the oil in a large frying pan over a medium heat. Add the mustard seeds and sauté for 2 minutes, or until they start to pop (they'll sound a bit like popcorn); be careful not to burn them. Add the onions and sauté for 3–5 minutes, or until soft and brown.

Stir in the garlic, ginger, curry leaves, cumin, fennel seeds, dill seeds and chilli powder and cook for 30 seconds. Add the seitan nuggets and cook for 2 minutes. Add the tomatoes, salt and 500 ml (2 cups) of water and cook for 15 minutes. Stir in the coconut milk, heat to a simmer and cook for 5 minutes.

Serve the curry with steamed rice and top with slices of chilli.

Serves 4

Sweet chilli barbecue seitan

Wheat gluten flour (sometimes called 'vital wheat gluten', or simply 'gluten flour') is the dried protein from wheat and makes a delicious meat alternative known as seitan. In this recipe, I slow-cook the seitan in chilli, malt and beer. Barley malt syrup can be found in some supermarkets and most health food stores. These flavours really come to life when the steaks are later seared on the barbecue or in a frying pan.

70 g (¼ cup) dark miso paste

3 garlic cloves, minced

2 tablespoons toasted sesame oil

2 tablespoons savoury yeast flakes

330 g (2¼ cups) wheat gluten flour

3 tablespoons rice bran oil, plus extra for grilling

1 tablespoon chilli flakes

3 garlic cloves, smashed

4 tablespoons barley malt syrup

2 tablespoons rice malt syrup

750 ml (3 cups) stout beer

salt and freshly ground black pepper

VEGAN

To make the seitan, dissolve the miso paste in 500 ml (2 cups) of water in a large bowl. Stir in the minced garlic and the sesame oil. Fold in the savoury yeast flakes and gluten flour and mix with a wooden spoon until a springy dough forms. Knead the dough in the bowl for 3 minutes. Set aside to rest for 10 minutes.

Divide the dough into 6 equal pieces. Place the first piece between 2 sheets of greaseproof paper and roll out with a rolling pin to a thickness of 3–4 cm. It will be quite springy and resist your efforts to shape it, but be persistent. Repeat with the remaining dough pieces. (They may look a bit small but they will expand during cooking.)

Heat the rice bran oil in a large casserole dish over a medium heat. Add the chilli flakes and smashed garlic. Cook for 30 seconds. Add the barley malt syrup, rice malt syrup and stout. Stir well. Add the seitan steaks. Reduce the heat to low, cover and simmer gently for 1 hour. It's important to cook the seitan slowly over a low heat otherwise it will expand and rise like bread, spoiling the end result. Remove the lid and cook for a further 30 minutes. If the liquid begins to dry up add 125 ml (½ cup) of water.

Remove the seitan with tongs and place in a colander to drain. Transfer the seitan to a plate and brush with oil.

Heat a heavy-based frying pan or barbecue plate over a medium heat. Add the seitan steaks and cook for 4–5 minutes on each side, or until browned. Season with salt and pepper and serve with a leafy green salad and barbecued potatoes.

Serves 6

Seitan in black bean sauce

This is a vegetarian adaptation of one of my Viennese grandma's favourite Chinese recipes, but despite the cultural fusion it totally works! The black beans in the recipe are actually fermented soy beans (available in packets or jars in Asian grocery stores), not black turtle beans. If you can't find them, use 4 tablespoons of black bean sauce. Seitan pieces are available at Suzy Spoon's Vegetarian Butcher (ha!), health food stores and Asian grocery stores, or you can make your own (see page 138).

2 teaspoons sugar

2 tablespoons soy sauce

2 tablespoons rice wine

3 teaspoons cornflour

2 tablespoons olive oil

2 teaspoons sesame oil

300 g seitan pieces

steamed rice, to serve

BLACK BEAN SAUCE

3 tablespoons rice bran oil

1 white onion, sliced

4 cm piece of ginger, peeled and finely chopped

4 garlic cloves, minced

1 tablespoon fermented black beans

1 red capsicum, sliced

1 tablespoon red miso paste

125 ml (½ cup) hot water

To make the marinade, combine the sugar, soy sauce, rice wine, cornflour, olive oil and sesame oil in a large bowl. Add the seitan and mix well, making sure all the seitan pieces are well coated with marinade. Cover and set aside.

For the sauce, heat the oil in a wok or large heavy-based frying pan over a medium–high heat. Add the onion and stir-fry for 3 minutes, or until translucent. Add the ginger and garlic and stir-fry for 1 minute. Add the black beans and capsicum and fry for 12 minutes. Finally, add the seitan and stir-fry for 3 minutes.

Mix the miso paste with the hot water and add to the wok. Stir-fry for 5 minutes.

Serve generous ladles of the seitan and sauce on steamed rice.

Serves 4

VEGAN

Crunchy seitan nuggets

Kids always love my crumbed seitan nuggets. I like to offer up a couple of different dipping sauces for them to try such as Simple Peanut Sauce (page 178) or Chunky Tomato Relish (page 176). These nuggets are also irresistible to adults, so keep plenty aside if you're feeding the little ones first. And if you don't have time to make your own, just use your favourite store-bought varieties (sweet chilli sauce or barbecue sauce are best).

4 tablespoons dark miso paste

3 garlic cloves, minced

2 tablespoons toasted sesame oil

2 tablespoons savoury yeast flakes

330 g (2¼ cups) wheat gluten flour

3 tablespoons soy sauce

1 bay leaf

75 g (½ cup) plain flour

250 ml (1 cup) milk

100 g (1 cup) breadcrumbs

1 litre (4 cups) rice bran oil, for frying

In a large bowl dissolve the miso paste in 500 ml (2 cups) of water. Stir in the garlic and sesame oil. Fold in the savoury yeast flakes and gluten flour. Mix with a wooden spoon until a springy dough forms. Knead in the bowl for 3 minutes. Cover and set aside to rest for 10 minutes.

Hold the dough in one hand and tear off a 3 cm piece. (The nuggets will expand when cooking so make them slightly smaller than your ideal nugget size.) Repeat with the remaining seitan.

In a large saucepan or stockpot, bring 2 litres of water to the boil over a medium heat. When simmering, add the soy sauce, bay leaf and seitan nuggets. Reduce the heat and simmer gently on low for 1½ hours, adding another 125 ml (½ cup) of water if too much liquid evaporates. Remove the nuggets with a slotted spoon and allow to cool in a colander. (Cooling the nuggets stops them from sweating which makes the crumbs soggy.)

Place the flour in a shallow bowl, the milk in small bowl and the breadcrumbs in another shallow bowl.

One by one, roll each nugget in the flour, dip it into the milk, and roll it in the breadcrumbs. Repeat until all the nuggets are crumbed.

Heat the oil in a large wok or heavy-based pan over a medium–high heat until the oil reaches 180°C. (You can tell the oil is ready if it bubbles around the end of a clean wooden spoon or chopstick when you dip it in.)

Cook the nuggets in batches (depending on the size of your wok or pan), for 3–4 minutes, or until brown and crunchy all over. Drain on paper towel. Sprinkle with a little salt and serve immediately with your favourite dipping sauces.

Serves 4

Seitan makhani

This is a vegetarian version of the classic Indian dish, chicken makhani (butter chicken). When I make it at home I use a plain soy yoghurt, but it's just as delicious using plain dairy yoghurt. You can make your own seitan (see page 138) but it's also available at Asian grocers, health food shops or from my vegetarian butcher!

600 g seitan pieces or nuggets

3 teaspoons garam masala

1½ teaspoons ground turmeric

1 teaspoon ground cumin

1 cup plain yoghurt

110 ml (scant ½ cup) olive oil

2 teaspoons finely chopped ginger

2 garlic cloves, finely chopped

½ teaspoon crushed cardamom seeds

2 cloves

1 teaspoon ground coriander

1 teaspoon chilli flakes

1 tablespoon lime juice

275 ml tomato purée

steamed rice, to serve

coriander leaves

MARINADE

2 garlic cloves, minced

2 teaspoons grated ginger

pinch of salt

½ teaspoon ground chilli

1 tablespoon lime juice

To make the marinade, combine all the ingredients in a large bowl. Add the seitan pieces and massage until well-coated. Cover and refrigerate for 15 minutes.

Preheat the oven to 180°C.

Remove the seitan from the fridge and add 1 teaspoon of the garam masala, ½ teaspoon of the turmeric and all of the cumin. Stir in half of the yoghurt and mix well, ensuring all of the seitan is coated.

Pour 4 tablespoons of the olive oil into a baking dish. Add the seitan and bake for 10 minutes. Turn the seitan and bake for another 10 minutes, or until the marinade begins to dry out a little.

Meanwhile, heat the remaining 1½ tablespoons of olive oil in a large frying pan over a medium–high heat. Add the ginger and garlic and sauté for 1 minute. Add the cardamom, cloves, ground coriander, chilli flakes, lime juice and remaining garam masala and turmeric. Stir well and cook for another 1–2 minutes, or until aromatic. Add the tomato puree, remaining yoghurt and seitan pieces and cook for a further 10 minutes.

Serve the seitan makhani with steamed rice and top with coriander leaves.

Serves 4

Seitan fillets with cream cheese and silverbeet

This dish is perfect for a romantic dinner. There's quite a bit of effort involved in making the seitan from scratch, but the taste and texture are absolutely worth it, plus your special someone will know just how much they are loved. It's important to take your time while massaging the seitan dough in water, as this process washes away all the carbs from the flour to leave just the wheat protein and produce pure seitan. And when you are rolling out the fillets, the seitan will be very springy, but persist in rolling it, as it will expand during cooking.

2 kg plain flour, plus 150 g (1 cup) extra for dusting

3 tablespoons rice bran oil

3 tablespoons red miso paste

4 silverbeet leaves, central stalks removed, diced

2 cups boiling water

150 g cream cheese

¼ teaspoon salt

250 ml (1 cup) milk

200 g (2 cups) breadcrumbs

Place the flour in a large bowl with 250 ml (1 cup) of water. Mix to make a firm dough. Knead in the bowl for about 2 minutes. Cover with water and set aside for 15 minutes.

Place the bowl in the sink, and gently massage the dough in the water until the water turns white and milky. Discard the milky water and add enough fresh cold water to the bowl to cover the dough. Repeat the massaging, draining and refilling process until the water runs clear (about 15–20 minutes). The dough will have reduced to about a third of its original size. Divide it into 2 pieces and use a rolling pin to flatten each one into a 'fillet' shape.

Preheat the oven to 120°C.

Heat the oil in a large frying pan over a medium–high heat. Add the fillets and cook for 4 minutes on each side, or until golden. Remove from the heat and set aside. Reserve the oil.

Dissolve the miso paste in 2 litres of water in a deep baking dish. Add the seitan fillets and poach, uncovered in the oven for 1 hour.

Place the silverbeet in a colander over the sink. Pour the boiling water over it. Place the wilted silverbeet, cream cheese and salt in a small bowl and mix well.

Remove the seitan from the baking dish. Cut into the long side of each fillet and spoon in the silverbeet and cheese filling.

Sprinkle the extra 150 g (1 cup) of flour on a small plate. Pour the milk into a bowl and spread the breadcrumbs on another small plate. Coat each fillet in the flour, dip it in the milk and then roll it in the breadcrumbs, coating evenly.

Reheat the oil in the pan over a medium heat and cook the fillets for 7–9 minutes each side, or until golden brown. Serve with salad.

Serves 2

Seitan roulade

This roulade makes a brilliant centrepiece for a dinner party or special occasion. We make a variation of this recipe at my shop for Christmas and it is very popular! But this recipe is not for the faint-hearted – it's a serious culinary enterprise, so give yourself plenty of time to read through the method before you start assembling your ingredients. You'll also need a rolling pin, cheesecloth, string and a large steamer.

FILLING

50 g (¼ cup) pearl barley

2 tablespoons olive oil

1 onion, finely diced

45 g button mushrooms, finely diced

90 g (about 3 slices) of day-old sourdough bread, cut into 1½cm cubes

1 garlic clove, minced

3 tablespoons chopped flat-leaf parsley leaves

1 tablespoon finely chopped sage leaves

2 teaspoons finely chopped rosemary leaves

2 teaspoons finely chopped thyme leaves

2½ tablespoons raisins

3 tablespoons roughly chopped walnuts

2 tablespoons sesame oil

pinch of salt

To make the filling, place the pearl barley in a saucepan with 1 litre (4 cups) of water and bring to the boil over a medium–high heat. Reduce the heat and simmer for 30–40 minutes, or until tender. Drain and set aside to cool.

Heat 2 tablespoons of oil in a large frying pan over a medium heat. Add the onion and sauté for 5–7 minutes until translucent. Add the mushrooms and cook for 10 minutes, or until softened. Add the bread and garlic and sauté for another 10 minutes, stirring often. Set aside to cool.

Once cool, transfer the onion, mushroom and bread mixture to a large mixing bowl. Add the pearl barley, garlic, parsley, sage, rosemary, thyme, raisins, walnuts, sesame oil and salt. Mix until well combined.

To make the seitan dough, combine the gluten flour and plain flour in a large mixing bowl. Add the yeast flakes, sage, rosemary, thyme, salt and pepper. Mix well and set aside.

In a small bowl dissolve the miso paste in the tepid water. Transfer to a food processor along with the olive oil, soy sauce and onion. Add the garlic and tofu and blend until well combined.

Transfer the contents of the food processor to the large bowl of flour and herbs. Mix with your hands to form springy dough. Turn the dough out onto a clean surface and use a rolling pin to flatten it into a 20 × 30 cm rectangle.

INGREDIENTS CONTINUED OVER PAGE

RECIPE CONTINUED OVER PAGE

Seitan roulade (cont.)

SEITAN DOUGH

150 g (1 heaped cup) wheat gluten flour

3 tablespoons plain flour

2 tablespoons savoury yeast flakes

1½ tablespoons finely chopped sage leaves

2 teaspoons finely chopped rosemary leaves

2 teaspoons finely chopped thyme leaves

½ teaspoon salt

½ teaspoon freshly ground black pepper

1 tablespoon white miso paste

100 ml tepid water

1¾ tablespoons olive oil

3 teaspoons soy sauce

½ onion, roughly chopped

2 garlic cloves, minced

150 g silken tofu

1 sheet of ready-made puff pastry

Spoon the filling onto the seitan dough, leaving a 1 cm border around the perimeter. Beginning from one of the short sides, roll up the seitan and filling to make a roulade. Pinch the short end to seal. Wrap the roulade in a 60 x 40 cm piece of cheesecloth and tie it with kitchen string at 5–6 cm intervals.

Bring 2–3 litres of water to the boil in a large steamer over a high heat. Place the roulade in the steamer and steam for 1 hour. Remove the roulade from the steamer and allow it to cool for 10 minutes before discarding the cheesecloth.

Meanwhile, preheat the oven to 180°C and grease a baking tray.

Place the roulade on the baking tray. Lay the pastry over the top and tuck the edges underneath, pressing them together if they overlap. Bake for 40 minutes, or until the pastry is golden.

Slice and serve hot with a leafy green salad or roast veggies.

Serves 6

Vegetable dishes

Barbecued field mushrooms

This is one of those recipes that proves the theory 'less is more'. Big field mushrooms don't need much to bring out their amazing natural flavours. If you haven't barbecued them before, *please* try this recipe. (If it's winter and you don't fancy standing outside, just bake them in the oven.)

6 large field mushrooms

60 ml (¼ cup) olive oil

120 ml seeded mustard

salt and freshly ground black pepper

GLUTEN-FREE

VEGAN

De-stem the mushrooms and slice off the tops so that they are flat on the top and bottom. Place cut-side down on a tray or shallow dish.

To make the marinade, place the oil and mustard in a small bowl or jug and whisk until well combined. Spoon the marinade over each mushroom, making sure the whole underside is covered. Sprinkle with salt and pepper, cover and refrigerate for 1 hour.

Heat a barbecue hotplate over a medium heat. Arrange the mushrooms on the hotplate and cook for 10 minutes on each side, or until aromatic, browned and crispy.

To cook in the oven, preheat the oven to 180°C. Place the mushrooms on a large oven tray and bake for 30 minutes or until the mushrooms have shrunk and are nicely caramelised.

Serves 6 as a side

Roasted brussels sprouts

The Brussels sprout is a much-maligned vegetable, and we all know people who claim to hate them with a vengeance. However, I'm betting they've only tried them boiled to mush. These little gems are sweet, crispy and *very* moreish. They make a delicious snack or a brilliant side dish for Seitan Fillets with Cream Cheese and Silverbeet (page 138).

1 kg Brussels sprouts

2 tablespoons olive oil, plus extra for serving

¼ teaspoon salt

¼ teaspoon freshly ground black pepper

GLUTEN-FREE

VEGAN

Preheat the oven to 180°C.

Trim the sprouts, removing the stumps and any loose or damaged leaves. Rinse them in a colander and pat dry with a clean tea-towel. Slice them in half lengthways and spread them over the base of a baking dish in a single layer. Drizzle over the olive oil and season with salt and pepper.

Roast the sprouts for 40 minutes, or until they are soft and some of the edges are golden. Transfer to a serving platter, drizzle with olive oil and season again.

Serves 4 as a side

Flame-cooked chilli corn

Who doesn't love corn on the cob? And the chilli flakes in this recipe add a nice depth. Cook them over a campfire for even greater deliciousness.

4 corn cobs with husks still on

4 tablespoons olive oil

2 teaspoons paprika

pinch of chilli powder

¼ teaspoon salt

tiny pinch of freshly ground black pepper

GLUTEN-FREE

VEGAN

De-husk the corn, retaining the husks and discarding the silks. Use a pastry brush to brush each cob with 1 tablespoon of oil. Sprinkle with paprika, salt, pepper and chilli flakes.

Wrap the cobs back up in their husks. Keep 1 husk leaf aside and tear 4 long strips from this leaf lengthways. Tie the husks to each cob using either these strips or kitchen string that has been soaked in water.

Heat a barbecue plate over a medium heat (or heat a campfire grill over a fire with plenty of embers). Place the cobs on top and cook for 15–20 minutes, turning every 5 minutes, or until the husks are dark and crispy.

Peel off the husks and serve immediately. Corn is a delicious side for veggie sausages or Sage and Garlic Bean Burgers (page 106).

Serves 4 as a side

Salt and pepper mushrooms

These crisp, peppery mushrooms are a great addition to a dinner party spread. Make sure you serve them with a big salad to balance out the fried goodness. A platter of these at a party or barbecue will disappear in seconds! Szechuan pepper is not strictly a pepper, but the zingy berries from the prickly ash tree. It should be easy to find in most supermarkets or Asian grocers.

500 g tiny button mushrooms

300 g (1¾ cups) rice flour

2½ tablespoons salt

2 tablespoons ground Szechuan pepper

½ teaspoon chilli powder

½ teaspoon garlic powder (optional)

4 tablespoons sesame seeds

500 ml (2 cups) sparkling mineral water

1 litre (4 cups) sunflower oil

GLUTEN-FREE

VEGAN

Trim the mushroom stems so they are flush with the caps.

In a large bowl combine the rice flour, salt, Szechuan pepper, chilli powder, garlic powder (if using) and sesame seeds. Mix well. Add the mineral water and stir to form a smooth batter.

Heat the oil to 180°C in a deep, heavy-based pan over a medium heat. (You can tell the oil is ready if it bubbles around the end of a clean wooden spoon or chopstick when you dip it in.)

Dip the mushrooms individually into the batter using a fork, making sure they are well coated then carefully drop them into the hot oil. Cook for 3–5 minutes until golden and crispy. Drain well on paper towel.

Serve hot with a leafy green salad.

Serves 6 as a starter

Roasted pumpkin with couscous and almonds

If you are looking for a dish to take to a picnic or barbecue, this salad looks beautiful, is easy to make and is guaranteed to please. Pearl couscous is also known as moghrabieh or Israeli couscous. It is a type of large couscous and is available from delicatessens and Middle Eastern food stores.

185 g (1 cup) pearl couscous (Israeli couscous)

600 g peeled pumpkin, cut into 4 cm chunks

2 tablespoons caramelised balsamic vinegar

80 ml (⅓ cup) olive oil

1 tablespoon red wine vinegar

juice of ¼ lemon

salt and freshly ground black pepper

2 spring onions, sliced

80 g (½ cup) roasted almonds, roughly chopped

VEGAN

Place the pearl couscous and 250 ml (1 cup) of water in a small saucepan and bring to the boil over high heat. Reduce the heat to medium–low, cover and cook for 10 minutes, or until all of the water has evaporated and the couscous is tender.

Preheat the oven to 180°C. Grease a large baking tray.

Place the balsamic vinegar and 2 tablespoons of the olive oil in a large bowl and whisk until well combined. Add the pumpkin and toss with a wooden spoon until the pieces are well coated. Spread the pumpkin on the baking tray and roast for 30 minutes, or until browned and beginning to caramelise.

To make the dressing, place the remaining 2 tablespoons of olive oil in a small jug or bowl. Whisk in the red wine vinegar, lemon juice and season with salt and pepper.

Transfer the couscous to a large serving bowl. Mix in the spring onions and almonds then add the roast pumpkin. Pour over the red wine dressing and toss to combine.

Serve immediately.

Serves 8 as a side

Layered vegetable tian

This recipe has it all. It's easy, healthy, quick to prepare and looks amazing. Tian refers both to the glazed terracotta baking dish that the French use for this traditional recipe, and also to the recipe itself, which involves layered ingredients baked in the oven.

2 zucchinis, sliced

4 yellow squash, sliced into rounds

1 red onion, sliced into rings

2 tomatoes, sliced into rounds

1 baguette loaf, sliced thinly

300 g desiree or pontiac potatoes, sliced into thin rounds

2 garlic cloves, finely chopped

10 sprigs of thyme

3 tablespoons olive oil

salt and freshly ground black pepper

VEGAN

Preheat the oven to 170°C. Grease a deep, rectangular baking tin or casserole dish.

Start at one end of the dish, arranging the vegetable slices in rows, alternating slices of zucchini, squash, onion, tomato, bread and potato until you have filled the dish.

Sprinkle over the garlic and thyme sprigs and drizzle over the olive oil. Season the veggies with a good pinch of salt and a couple of twists of freshly ground black pepper. Bake for 45 minutes or until the veggies are cooked and beginning to caramelise. Serve immediately. This dish would go well with my Seitan Roulade (page 151) or Pan-fried Chilli Tempeh (page 124).

Serves 6 as a side

Viennese dumplings in mushroom goulash

My great grandmother brought this recipe to Sydney from Vienna in 1931. It's a family favourite, and brings back memories of a loving house filled with the aroma of apple strudel and dumplings.

60 ml (¼ cup) olive oil

2 large onions, diced

25 g (¼ cup) sweet paprika

1 tablespoon white vinegar

4 garlic cloves, minced

400 g button mushrooms

2 tablespoons tomato paste

2 teaspoons salt

1 loaf sourdough bread

60 g butter, melted

1 teaspoon salt

250 ml (1 cup) milk

1 tablespoon plain flour

75 g (½ cup) self-raising flour

Heat the oil in a large saucepan over a medium heat. Add the onions and sauté for 3–5 minutes or until soft and transparent. Remove from the heat and quickly stir in the paprika so as not to burn it. Add the vinegar and 125 ml (½ cup) of water. Return the pan to the stove and reduce the heat to low. Add the garlic, mushrooms, tomato paste and salt and simmer for 3–4 minutes. Add 500 ml (2 cups) of water. Simmer for 30 minutes, or until the liquid has reduced and thickened. (Add 1–3 tablespoons of water if it is too thick. The gravy needs to be thick but plentiful.)

Meanwhile, to make the dumplings cut the crusts off the bread so that you are left with about 400 g. Cut the bread into small cubes and place them in a large bowl. Add the butter, salt and milk and mix well. Allow to soak for 5 minutes.

Sift the flours into a small bowl. Add the flours to the bread cubes and stir them through. Using wet hands shape the mixture into balls (a bit smaller than tennis balls), squeezing them tightly so they don't fall apart.

In a large saucepan, bring 2 litres of water to the boil over a medium–high heat. Drop the dumplings into the water and return to the boil. Reduce the heat to low and simmer gently for 20 minutes, or until the dumplings are cooked.

Remove the dumplings with a slotted spoon and divide between 6 serving bowls. Pour over the goulash and serve.

Serves 6

Crispy crumbed eggplant

There's something deeply satisfying about this simple dish. Every bite of the crispy crumbed shell gives way to the surprisingly soft eggplant inside. This is delicious with Lemon and Coriander Dipping Sauce (page 172). The recipe is also easily adapted for vegans and those with gluten-intolerance.

150 g (1 cup) flour

250 ml (1 cup) milk

100 g (1 cup) breadcrumbs

750 g (2 large) eggplant, cut into 1 cm thick slices

250 ml (1 cup) rice bran oil, for frying

salt

Place the flour on a plate, the milk in a bowl and the breadcrumbs on another plate and set them side by side.

Use a fork to dip each slice of eggplant alternately into the flour, milk and breadcrumbs, making sure both sides are coated. Place on a large plate or platter. Repeat until all the eggplant is crumbed.

Heat the oil in a deep, heavy-based frying pan over a medium–high heat until the oil reaches 180°C. (You can tell the oil is ready if it bubbles around the end of a clean wooden spoon or chopstick when you dip it in.) Fry the eggplant in batches for about 3–5 minutes each side, or until crisp and browned. Sprinkle with salt and serve immediately.

Serves 6 as a starter

Jerusalem artichokes with spinach, lemon and thyme

Jerusalem artichokes are actually no relation to artichokes but are a species of sunflower – you eat the tuberous root, which is a bit like a sweet, nutty spud. They'd always copped a bad rap in my family (my grandfather grew up in the depression, and sometimes that's all there was for dinner). I was told that they tasted like ants (!) so I didn't try them until I was in my twenties. Now I *love* them, especially baked, as it makes the most of their delicious flavour.

500 g Jerusalem artichokes

2 tablespoons olive oil

salt and freshly ground black pepper

200 g (4 cups firmly packed) baby spinach leaves

750 ml (3 cups) boiling water

½ lemon

1 teaspoon thyme leaves, plus extra thyme sprigs, to serve

GLUTEN-FREE

VEGAN

Preheat the oven to 180°C.

Arrange the whole, washed artichokes in a heavy-based baking dish. Add the oil and a pinch each of salt and pepper. Rub the oil and seasoning all over the artichokes. Bake them in the oven for 40 minutes, or until the skin is browned and crispy. Remove from the oven.

Place the spinach in a colander over the sink. Carefully pour over the boiling water to wilt the spinach. Drain well.

Transfer the spinach to serving plates and top with the artichokes. Squeeze over the lemon juice and scatter over the thyme leaves and sprigs. Serve immediately with a green leafy salad. It would also go well with my Chickpea Salad with Loads of Herbs (page 54).

Serves 4 as a side

Spiced red cabbage and peas

This colourful dish tastes as good as it looks. Use fresh peas if they are available, but frozen peas are fine (and incidentally, are equally nutritious). If you don't have tortillas, you can also serve the spiced cabbage on rice or some lovely toasted sourdough.

80 ml (⅓ cup) rice bran oil

½ teaspoon turmeric

salt

2–3 chat potatoes (about 130 g in total), chopped into small cubes

1 onion, finely chopped

1 bay leaf

½ teaspoon ground cumin

½ teaspoon minced ginger

¼ teaspoon chilli powder

4 tomatoes, chopped

75 g (1 cup) finely sliced red cabbage

150 g (1 cup) peas

2 tortillas, to serve

VEGAN

Heat 3 tablespoons of the oil in a heavy-based frying pan over a medium heat. Add the turmeric and a pinch of salt and sauté for 3–4 seconds. Add the potatoes and cook for 5–10 minutes keeping them moving in the pan so they are well-seasoned. Remove potatoes from the heat, transfer to a bowl and set aside to cool.

Wipe out the pan with paper towel, add the remaining oil and reheat the pan over a medium heat. Add the onion and sauté for 3–5 minutes until soft. Stir through the bay leaf, cumin, ginger, chilli powder and tomatoes and cook for 10 minutes. Add the cabbage and stir until well-covered in spices. Cover and cook on low for 3–5 minutes. Add the peas and potatoes and another pinch of salt. Cover and cook for 10–15 minutes, or until the potatoes are soft.

Spoon the cabbage mix onto the tortillas, roll up and serve immediately.

Serves 2

Suzy's

Condiments and dressings

Hot chilli jam

This delicious condiment is my absolute favourite, and makes a lovely gift. The jam will last a few months when refrigerated, but would never last that long in my house! Wear disposable gloves while chopping the chillies as there are so many of them and we're keeping the seeds. You'll need to simmer the jam for 12 hours, so make sure you allow plenty of time. You will need about five 250 ml jars with lids to store the jam.

1.2 kg long red chillies, roughly chopped

6 onions, roughly chopped

10 garlic cloves, peeled

750 ml (3 cups) olive oil

zest of 2 limes

2 cinnamon sticks

6 green apples, peeled, cored and diced

1 kg tomatoes, diced

juice of 5 limes

200 g (1 cup) brown sugar

GLUTEN-FREE

VEGAN

Place the chilli, onions, garlic, oil and lime zest in a food processor and process for about 1 minute, or until smooth.

Pour the chilli and onion puree into a heavy-based saucepan and place over a medium heat. Add the cinnamon sticks, apples, tomatoes and 200 ml of water. Cover and cook at a low simmer for 10 hours, stirring regularly.

Add the lime juice and sugar and simmer for a further 2 hours.

Meanwhile, to sterilise the jars, preheat the oven to 160°C. Wash the jars and lids thoroughly in warm, soapy water and rinse. Place the still-wet jars (not the lids) on a baking tray and heat in the oven for 10 minutes. Remove the tray and cover with a clean tea-towel. Place the lids in a small saucepan of water and simmer for 10 minutes. Remove from the heat and cover until ready to use.

Spoon the jam into the sterilised jars. Use tongs to remove the lids from the pan and dry them with the clean tea-towel. Seal the jars. Turn the jars upside down so the hot sticky jam seals the lid as it cools.

Makes 1.5 kg (about 5 cups)

CONDIMENTS AND DRESSINGS

MacDonnas' vegan mayo

People always ask me for this mayo recipe. We served it on our burgers at MacDonnas (the burger restaurant I owned in the 1990s), and it's actually quite simple. Its creamy, smoothness comes from the silken tofu, its amazing colour from the basil, and its zing from the garlic and lemon juice. Use it as a dip for veggie sticks, or a delicious topping for steamed vegetables.

300 g silken tofu

2 tablespoons seeded mustard

juice of 1 large lemon (about 3 tablespoons)

4 garlic cloves, peeled

¼ teaspoon salt

¼ teaspoon freshly ground black pepper

3 large handfuls of basil leaves

125 ml (½ cup) olive oil

GLUTEN-FREE

VEGAN

Combine all the ingredients (except the oil) in a food processor and pulse until the basil leaves have broken down then process until smooth. Keep the processor running and slowly add the oil in a constant drizzle until the mixture is creamy. Turn off the processor when you are sure all the oil is combined.

This delicious mayo keeps in an airtight container in the fridge for about 7 days.

Makes 500 g (about 2 cups)

Creamy almond and soy dressing

This delicious dressing is perfect for a potato salad instead of mayonnaise. Try a dollop on baked potatoes – dreamy!

160 g (1 cup) almonds

2 garlic cloves, peeled

250 ml (1 cup) soy milk

1 tablespoon soy milk powder

1 teaspoon white vinegar

juice of 2 lemons

500 ml (2 cups) olive oil

salt and freshly ground black pepper

GLUTEN-FREE

VEGAN

Place the almonds in a food processor and blitz for 20 seconds until coarsely ground. Add the garlic, soy milk, soy milk powder, vinegar and lemon juice and process until smooth.

Place the oil in a jug. Turn on the processor and slowly pour in a thin stream of oil until the mixture is smooth and creamy. Season to taste with salt and pepper. Add a drop of water if the cream is too thick for you.

This dressing will last for 7–8 days if stored in an airtight container in the fridge.

Makes 550 g (3 cups)

Roasted almond butter

Almond butter is tasty, nutritious and an absolute staple in our house. We use it as a spread for toast, sandwiches and wraps; as a base for dressings; and as a magic ingredient in cakes, biscuits and desserts. It's quite expensive to buy so it's worth making your own with the freshest almonds you can find. Feel free to process the almonds raw if you prefer, but I rather like the richness of roasted almonds.

320 g (2 cups) almonds
sea salt
3 tablespoons coconut oil, melted

GLUTEN FREE

VEGAN

Preheat the oven to 150°C. Line a baking tray with greaseproof paper.

Spread the almonds on the tray so they're not overlapping. Roast them for 10–12 minutes (check them often as they are easily burnt).

Transfer the almonds to a food processor or blender and process on low until they begin to give up their oil. (You need a low setting because at higher speeds, the almond pulp will stick to the sides.) This may take 10 minutes or longer. Use a fork to stir the almond meal regularly so it doesn't cake up. Add the coconut oil, 1 tablespoon at a time, until the almonds have the consistency of peanut butter.

Spoon the almond butter into a jar or container with a lid and refrigerate. It should last for up to 4 weeks.

Makes 310 g (1 cup)

Lemon and coriander dipping sauce

This sweet and sour dipping sauce is perfect for Golden Tempeh Fingers (page 120), spring rolls, curry puffs or almost any savoury party food. I've even used it as a dressing on a crunchy cabbage and noodle salad and it was fantastic. For a hotter sauce, retain the chilli seeds.

200 g (1 cup) brown sugar

¼ teaspoon salt

juice of 1 lemon

1 teaspoon lemon zest

1 large red cayenne chilli, deseeded and finely chopped

2 tablespoons chopped coriander leaves

Heat 150 ml of water in a saucepan over a medium heat. Add the sugar and cook for 5 minutes, or until the mixture begins to caramelise and thicken. Remove from the heat and allow to cool for 10 minutes. Add the salt, lemon juice, lemon zest, chilli and coriander and stir well. Cool before serving.

This sauce can be stored in a sealed container in the fridge for up to 1 week.

Makes 250 ml (1 cup)

Sesame and lime dressing

A dressing that will become a favourite; not only because it adds a zing to almost anything, but it's so easy you can make it in minutes. Tahini is a paste made from crushed sesame seeds, either hulled or unhulled. I use the hulled type for this recipe because it has a milder flavour and is a lighter colour.

juice of 1 lime (about 2 tablespoons)

3 tablespoons hulled tahini

1 tablespoon soy sauce

Combine the lime juice and tahini in a small bowl. Add the soy sauce and 3 tablespoons of water and stir well.

Drizzle this dressing over Mung Bean, Brown Rice and Zucchini Balls (page 100), barbecued tofu or any kind of salad.

Makes 125 ml (½ cup)

LEMON AND CORIANDER DIPPING SAUCE (PICTURED)

Spiced eggplant dip

This scrumptious eggplant dip has a creamy texture and a cheeky bite, thanks to the garam masala, garlic, chilli and ginger. It's great with rice or buckwheat crackers, corn bread or other gluten-free options.

3 tablespoons olive oil

1 large red onion, diced

3 garlic cloves, minced

4 cm piece of ginger, peeled and grated

1 teaspoon garam masala

½ teaspoon ground turmeric

½ teaspoon chilli flakes

2 large eggplants, diced

2 large ripe tomatoes, diced

2 teaspoons salt

GLUTEN-FREE

VEGAN

Heat the oil in a large, heavy-based frying pan over a medium heat. Sauté the onion for 3–5 minutes, or until it is soft and translucent. Add the garlic and ginger and sauté for 1 minute. Add the spices and sauté for another minute before adding the eggplant and tomato. Reduce the heat, cover and cook for 1 hour, stirring frequently.

Serve hot with vegetables or cold as a dip. Store in an airtight container in the fridge – it will keep for 3–4 days.

Makes about 1 kg (5 cups)

Chunky tomato relish

This is a delectable relish that goes well with just about any savoury meal! It makes a lovely Christmas gift, and is a great way to use up that summer abundance of tomatoes. You'll need a couple of sterilised jars to store the relish (it will last for 3 to 4 months sealed in the fridge). Feel free to buy new jars, but it's equally fine to re-use old jars as long as the rubber seal in the lids is in good nick. (I explain how to sterilise the jars below.)

2 red onions, diced

4 garlic cloves, minced

2 kg tomatoes, diced

125 ml (½ cup) apple cider vinegar

1 teaspoon chilli flakes

1 tablespoon salt

1½ teaspoons freshly ground black pepper

3 tablespoons olive oil

400 g (2 cups) brown sugar

GLUTEN-FREE

VEGAN

Place all the ingredients (except the sugar) in a large saucepan or stockpot over a medium heat and bring to the boil. Reduce the heat to low and simmer gently for 1 hour, stirring regularly, until the liquid thickens and darkens. Add the sugar and simmer for another 30 minutes.

Meanwhile, preheat the oven to 160°C. Wash the jars and lids thoroughly in warm, soapy water and rinse. Place the still-wet jars (not the lids) on a baking tray and heat in the oven for 10 minutes. Remove the tray and cover with a clean tea-towel. Place the lids in a small saucepan of water and simmer for 10 minutes. Remove from the heat and cover until ready to use.

Spoon the relish into the sterilised jars. Remove the lids from the pan with tongs and dry with the clean tea-towel before sealing the jars.

Serve this relish with mung bean cakes, seitan kebabs, tofu nuggets, burger patties or any savoury dish.

Makes about 840 g (3 cups)

Garlic bread dip

A simple and tasty way to use up leftover garlic bread or day-old bread. You can serve this with fresh sticks of cucumber, carrot, celery or capsicum for a great snack or starter.

80 g (½ cup) almonds

300 g leftover garlic bread or 1 French baguette

1 garlic clove, minced

10 g (½ cup) flat-leaf parsley leaves

salt and freshly ground black pepper

2½ tablespoons apple cider vinegar

3 tablespoons olive oil

Place the almonds in a food processor and blitz to a fine meal (about 30 seconds, depending on your processor). Add the bread, garlic and 750 ml (3 cups) of water and process for another 30 seconds until thick, smooth and well combined. Add the parsley, salt and pepper and process again for about 30 seconds, or until blended. With the food processor running, carefully add the vinegar and oil in a thin stream and process until creamy.

Makes about 750 ml (3 cups)

Simple peanut sauce

A spicy sauce with endless possibilities! Spoon it over steamed veggies, spread it on a tofu burger or serve it with Golden Tempeh Fingers (page 120). I often use it as an 'instant marinade' and spoon it over skewered vegetables or anything else I'm cooking on the barbecue.

3 tablespoons peanut butter

2 tablespoons soy sauce

2 tablespoons lime juice

2 garlic cloves, minced

1 small red chilli, finely diced

2 tablespoons sweet chilli sauce

180 ml (¾ cup) coconut milk

Combine all the ingredients in a saucepan and place over a medium heat. Add 3 tablespoons of water and stir well. Simmer for 10 minutes until the sauce thickens and darkens slightly. Serve hot or cold.

Makes 300 g (1 cup)

Pickled okra

Okra is a nutritious little veggie. It's high in vitamin C, fibre, folate and minerals, and has a taste somewhere between asparagus and eggplant. It also becomes gelatinous when you slice it or cook it (I love the texture!) and is used as a thickening agent in just about every cuisine (African, Middle Eastern, South Asian and South American). Pickled okra is great in sandwiches and salads. Just slice it and use it as you would gherkins. These make a lovely gift, especially if you have nice preserving jars.

12 garlic cloves, sliced

4 whole red chillies

1 white onion, sliced into rings

2 tablespoons dill leaves

1 kg okra

1 litre (4 cups) white vinegar

90 g (⅓ cup) salt

GLUTEN-FREE

VEGAN

To sterilise your jars, preheat the oven to 160°C. Wash the jars and lids thoroughly in warm, soapy water and rinse. Place the still-wet jars (not the lids) on a baking tray and heat in the oven for 10 minutes. Remove the tray and cover with a clean tea towel. Place the lids in a small saucepan of water and simmer for 10 minutes. Remove from the heat and cover until ready to use.

Decoratively pack the jars with equal amounts of garlic, chilli, onion, dill and okra.

Pour the vinegar into a large saucepan and place over a medium–high heat. Add the salt and 500 ml (2 cups) of water and bring to the boil. Carefully pour the boiled liquid into the jars. Remove the lids from the sterilising water with tongs and dry with the clean tea towel. Place the lids on the jars (the heat from the pickling liquid will help seal the jars tight).

Allow the jars to cool completely then pop them in the fridge. (They need to stay in the fridge for 1 month before eating.) They will last for up to 4 months unopened. Once opened consume within 3–4 weeks.

Makes 4 x 200 g jars

Preserved asparagus

Preserved asparagus makes a great side dish or a lovely addition to a salad. I quite like it on toast for brunch. And of course, a jar of preserved anything makes a lovely handmade gift. The asparagus looks beautiful in the jars, keeps well and tastes divine.

1.25 litres white vinegar

1.25 kg asparagus

1 litre (4 cups) iced water

500 ml (2 cups) olive oil

4 garlic cloves, sliced

1 small chilli, deseeded and sliced

1½ teaspoons salt

8 peppercorns

sprigs of parsley

GLUTEN-FREE

VEGAN

For this recipe you will need 2 x 500 ml jars with lids. To sterilise your jars, preheat the oven to 160°C. Wash the jars and lids thoroughly in warm, soapy water and rinse. Place the jars (not the lids) on a baking tray and heat in the oven for 10 minutes. Remove the tray and cover with a clean tea-towel. Place the lids in a small saucepan of water and simmer for 10 minutes. Remove from the heat and cover until ready to use.

Pour the vinegar and 750 ml (3 cups) of water into a large saucepan. Place over a medium heat and bring to the boil.

Trim the woody ends of the asparagus and discard. Cut the spears evenly so that that tips and stalks are able to fit into your jars. Add the asparagus to the pan and simmer for 2 minutes.

Meanwhile, pour the iced water into a bowl. Use tongs to transfer the asparagus to the iced water. When cool, drain the asparagus on paper towel.

Combine the oil, garlic, chilli, salt and peppercorns in a large mixing bowl. Add the asparagus and gently rub over the oil and seasonings. Pour 2 tablespoons of the seasoned olive oil into the bottom of each jar. Carefully place the asparagus tips and stalks in the jars, with the spear-ends down. Divide the excess oil between the jars, making sure each jar gets garlic, peppercorns and chilli. Add a couple of sprigs of parsley to each jar. If the oil doesn't reach the top of the jar, add a little extra if necessary.

Use clean tongs to remove the jar lids from the saucepan of water. Dry with the clean tea-towel and seal jars. Refrigerate immediately.

Store the preserved asparagus in the fridge for at least 3 weeks before opening. It will keep for up to 5 months refrigerated in sealed jars, and for about 2 weeks once open.

Makes 2 x 500 ml jars

Suzy's

Desserts and puddings

Kiwifruit and lime sorbet

Your friends will be so excited when you make this homemade sorbet on a hot summer evening. I don't have an ice cream machine so I make it using the freeze-and-stir method. It's not that hard to do, especially if you are already in the kitchen whipping up something for main course. (Of course, use your ice cream maker if you have one!)

9 ripe kiwifruit, skin removed

300 g (1¼ cups) caster sugar

2 sprigs of mint

juice and zest of 1 lime

pulp of 1 passionfruit, to serve

GLUTEN-FREE

VEGAN

Place the kiwifruit and sugar in a food processor. Add the leaves of 1 sprig of mint, the lime juice and 1 teaspoon of the lime zest. Blend for 1 minute, or until smooth.

Transfer the kiwifruit mix to a plastic or stainless steel bowl and place in the freezer. Take the bowl out every 15 minutes and stir it vigorously with a fork to break up any icicles. This method can take up to 2–3 hours, depending on your freezer. Once you are happy with the consistency (in other words, it's icy and no longer 'sloppy') transfer the sorbet to a container with a lid and keep in the freezer until you are ready to serve.

Serve the sorbet with passionfruit pulp, fresh mint leaves and a sprinkling of lime zest.

Serves 4

Strawberry parfaits with pomegranate and pistachio

These decadent little parfaits are ideal for a dinner party and taste as delicious as they look. You'll need 6 small (about 120 ml) glasses for this recipe.

1 pomegranate

4 tablespoons white sugar

3 tablespoons cornflour

pinch of salt

300 g (2 cups) fresh strawberries, hulled

350 g silken tofu

75 g (½ cup) unsalted pistachios, shelled and crushed, plus 50 g (⅓ cup) extra pistachios, shelled

VEGAN

To juice the pomegranate cut it in half around its equator. Squeeze each half into a bowl. Tap the bottom of the pomegranate with a spoon to expel all the seeds into the bowl, removing any pith or flesh that may have fallen in. Strain the juice into a saucepan. Transfer the seeds to a sealed container and place in the fridge.

Add the sugar and 180 ml (¾ cup) of water to the pomegranate juice. Heat the saucepan over a medium–high heat until the sugar dissolves. Add the cornflour and salt and stir continuously until the liquid reaches a high simmer. Reduce the heat to low and cook, still stirring, for 30–60 seconds longer until the liquid is very thick. Set aside to cool.

Place the strawberries and tofu in a food processer and process until smooth. Add the cooled pomegranate syrup and blend until creamy.

Divide the crushed pistachios between the 6 glasses. Spoon the parfait mixture into each glass and refrigerate for 8 hours or overnight.

When ready to serve, top each parfait with whole pistachios and pomegranate seeds.

Serves 6

Tofu
and lime
cheesecake

This is a recipe from *Cooking Cleverly with Beverly*, my first cooking show on community TV. It got great feedback from viewers, who adored the crunchy biscuit base and creamy tofu lime filling. It's super easy to make a vegan version by using dairy-free spread and vegan cream cheese. I use Marie biscuits but there are plenty of vegan biscuits available at health food stores.

400 g plain sweet biscuits

250 g butter, melted

500 g silken tofu

250 g cream cheese

juice of 1 lime

1½ tablespoons blackstrap molasses

¼ teaspoon ground nutmeg

1 tablespoon lime zest

Preheat the oven to 180°C. Grease a shallow 28 cm round pie dish.

Place the biscuits in a food processor and process until coarsely crumbled. Pour in the melted butter and process again until the crumbs are fine and moist. Spoon the biscuit mixture into the pie dish and spread it evenly over the base and sides, pressing it down firmly with your fingers. Set aside.

Wash and rinse the processor bowl. Place the tofu, cream cheese, lime juice, molasses and nutmeg in the food processor and blitz for 30–60 seconds until smooth.

Pour the tofu filling over the pie crust and sprinkle the top with nutmeg. Bake for 20 minutes, or until the top and biscuit edges begin to brown.

Remove the cheesecake from the oven and allow to cool. Sprinkle the lime zest over the top and chill before serving. Store in an airtight cake container in the fridge and consume within 3 days.

Serves 8

Cashew and vanilla custard

This gorgeous dessert is easy to make and tastes delicious with its velvety cashew and vanilla custard and burst of sweet blueberries.

3 saffron threads

2 tablespoons warm water

260 g (1¾ cups) raw cashews

250 ml (1 cup) almond milk (for a recipe, see page 234)

80 g raw sugar

1 teaspoon lemon zest

1 vanilla pod, seeds scraped

125 g blueberries

GLUTEN-FREE

VEGAN

Preheat the oven to 190°C. Grease a 20 x 20 cm baking dish.

Infuse the saffron in the water in a small glass.

Place the cashews and almond milk in a food processor. Add 3 tablespoons of the sugar, the lemon zest and vanilla. Process for 60 seconds, or until thick and creamy. Add the saffron water and pulse to combine.

Transfer the mixture to the baking dish and sprinkle the top with the remaining sugar. Bake for 20 minutes, or until the sugar on top begins to brown.

Allow to cool, then chill in the fridge for at least 1 hour. Decorate the top with blueberries just before serving.

Serves 4

Apple crumble with banana cream

A delightful variation of a traditional apple crumble, this recipe is easily modified for the vegan palate. If you've never tried luscious banana cream, you're in for quite a treat!

8 granny smith apples, peeled, cored and cut into chunks

1 teaspoon lemon zest

3 tablespoons dark brown sugar

2 tablespoons wholemeal flour

60 g (¾ cup) rolled oats

30 g butter

1 tablespoon golden syrup

3 bananas, peeled and frozen

3–4 tablespoons milk

Preheat the oven to 180°C. Grease a 30 cm pie dish, or 6 x 7 cm ramekins.

Place the apples in a saucepan over a medium–low heat. Cover and cook for 10 minutes. Add the lemon zest and 1 tablespoon of the sugar and cook for a further 10 minutes. Spoon the apple mixture into the baking dish (or ramekins, if using).

To make the crumble topping, combine the flour and oats in a bowl. Rub the butter into the oats with your fingertips. Add the remaining sugar and the golden syrup and mix well.

Spoon the crumble over the apple and bake for 25–30 minutes, or until the top is crisp and golden.

Meanwhile, to make the banana cream, cut the frozen banana into chunks and place in the food processor. Add the milk and process until creamy. Transfer to a bowl and place in the fridge until the crumble is ready.

Serve the crumble with a generous dollop of banana cream.

Serves 6

Carob–tofu pie with cherry coulis

The earthy carob, soft tofu and crunchy roasted almonds create a delightful combination of textures and flavours in this rich pie. Vegans can simply use dairy-free spread instead of the butter, and sweet vegan biscuits are available from some supermarkets and most health food stores.

200 g plain sweet biscuits

160 g (1 cup) roasted almonds

250 g butter, cut into cubes

FILLING

160 g (1 cup) carob buttons

1 tablespoon butter

300 g silken tofu

110 g (½ cup) sugar

CHERRY COULIS

150 g fresh or frozen cherries, pitted

3 tablespoons caster sugar

Preheat the oven to 180°C. Grease a shallow 25 cm round pie dish.

Place the biscuits in a food processor and blitz until coarsely crumbled. Add the almonds and process to a fine meal. Add the butter and process until well combined.

Tip the biscuit mixture into the pie dish and press it firmly and evenly over the base and sides (the back of a tablespoon might help). Set aside.

Melt the carob and butter in a small saucepan over a low heat, stirring occasionally.

Place the tofu, sugar and melted carob mixture in the food processor and process until smooth.

Pour the tofu filling into the pie crust and bake for 30 minutes, or until the top of the pie is soft but firm. (Give the dish a little wobble to check that it is firm. If it's still a bit loose and wet, return to the oven for an extra 10 minutes.)

While the pie is cooking, make the cherry coulis. Place the cherries and sugar in a small saucepan with 2 tablespoons of water. Bring to the boil over a medium heat, then reduce the heat to medium–low and simmer for 3–4 minutes, or until the sugar has dissolved and the coulis has reduced and thickened slightly.

Once the pie is cooked, remove from the oven and allow to cool before slicing and serving with the cherry coulis.

Serves 8

Raspberry bake with quinoa and almond topping

Raspberries are such a special summer fruit and this sweet bake is a great way to celebrate their rich colour and flavour. Finished with a crunchy quinoa and almond topping, this dessert is sure to become a favourite. Vegans can use a non-dairy spread instead of butter and some dairy-free ice cream to serve.

180 ml (¾ cup) warm water

75 g brown sugar

100 g (½ cup) white quinoa, rinsed

2 tablespoons butter

750 g (6 cups) raspberries

1 tablespoon cornflour

3 tablespoons golden syrup

2 tablespoons lemon juice

1 vanilla pod, seeds scraped

3 tablespoons almond meal

3 tablespoons slivered almonds

ice cream, to serve

Place the warm water in a saucepan and add 2 tablespoons of the sugar, stirring until dissolved. Add the quinoa and bring to the boil over a high heat. Reduce the heat to low, cover and simmer for 15–20 minutes, or until the liquid is absorbed and the quinoa is fluffy and has little tails. Remove from the heat, stir in the butter, cover and set aside.

Preheat the oven to 180°C. Grease a 20 x 20 cm baking dish.

Place the raspberries in a large bowl with the cornflour, golden syrup, lemon juice, vanilla and remaining sugar. Mix well and spoon into the baking dish.

Transfer the quinoa to a large bowl and stir in the almond meal and almonds. Spoon the mixture over the raspberries.

Bake for 30–40 minutes, or until brown and crunchy on top. Serve with your favourite ice cream.

Serves 6

Kathy's chocolate self-saucing pudding

An irresistible, delightfully indulgent chocolate pudding that's so easy to make it will almost certainly become part of your repertoire. Vegan ice cream is available at most supermarkets. You can use your favourite jam in this recipe; I like to use strawberry jam because I love how it works with the chocolate.

60 g dairy-free spread

100 g (½ cup) brown sugar

1 tablespoon strawberry or raspberry jam

150 g (1 cup) self-raising flour

40 g (⅓ cup) cocoa, plus extra to to serve

pinch of salt

185 ml (¾ cup) soy milk

2 tablespoons icing sugar

vegan ice cream, to serve

SAUCE

3 tablespoons cocoa

100 g (½ cup) brown sugar

375 ml (1½ cups) boiling water

VEGAN

Preheat the oven to 180°C. Grease a deep pie dish.

Cream the dairy-free spread and brown sugar in a large bowl with a wooden spoon or electric mixer. Add the jam and stir well. Sift the flour, cocoa and salt into the bowl and mix. Stir in the soy milk a tablespoonful at a time. Pour the mixture into the pie dish.

To make the sauce, sprinkle the cocoa and brown sugar over the pudding mixture. Pour the boiling water over the back of a spoon onto the pudding. (This prevents the water hitting the cocoa and sugar too fast and spreading them unevenly over the surface.)

Bake the pudding for 45 minutes, or until the pudding is cooked and the sauce (which will now be at the bottom) is thick and sticky.

Remove from the oven, sift over some cocoa and serve hot with vegan ice cream.

Serves 6

Suzy's

Cakes, biscuits and sweet treats

Chunky choc chip and almond biscuits

For me this is the perfect biscuit – it has crunch, chunks of chocolate and roasted almonds – yum! If, like me, you like your chocolate biscuits really gnarly, you can leave the almonds whole and chop the chocolate into super-large chunks. For this recipe I use dairy-free spread and dairy-free chocolate, but if you don't mind dairy products, you can use butter and regular chocolate.

180 g (1¼ cups) wholemeal flour

1 teaspoon bicarbonate of soda

150 g (¾ cup) brown sugar

155 g (1 cup) roasted almonds, roughly chopped

180 g dairy-free spread, melted

2 tablespoons soy milk

200 g dark dairy-free chocolate, roughly chopped

VEGAN

Preheat the oven to 180°C. Grease and line a baking tray with greaseproof paper.

Sift the flour and bicarbonate of soda into a large bowl (tip in the husks after sifting). Stir in the sugar and almonds. Add the dairy-free spread and soy milk and mix gently with a wooden spoon. Stir in the chocolate.

Roll tablespoons of the mixture into balls and place on the baking tray, leaving space for spreading. Bake for 15–20 minutes, or until firm to the touch.

Remove from the oven. Allow to sit for 3 minutes before transferring to wire racks. Store in an airtight container or jar.

Makes 25 biscuits

Strawberry and apricot jam drops

Jam drops are brilliant for taking to birthday parties or other social occasions because they are quick to make and look so beautiful (like a plate of edible jewels!). I prefer to use strawberry or apricot jam, but any jam is delicious.

210 g dairy-free spread
110 g (½ cup) caster sugar
175 g (1¼ cups) plain flour
pinch of salt
jam of your choice

VEGAN

Preheat the oven to 180°C. Line 2 baking trays with greaseproof paper.

Beat the dairy-free spread and sugar in a large mixing bowl using a wooden spoon or an electric mixer until creamy and fluffy. Fold in the flour and salt and stir to form a rough dough.

Sprinkle flour over a smooth clean surface. Turn the dough out onto the floured surface and roll into a long, sausage shape about 4 cm in diameter. Cut the dough into 3 cm segments. Roll each segment into a ball.

Arrange the balls, evenly spaced, on the baking trays. Create a hole in the centre of each biscuit with your thumb and fill with your chosen jam.

Bake for 15 minutes, or until the bases of the biscuits begin to brown. Transfer to wire racks – they'll firm up as they cool.

Store the biscuits (if there are any left!) in an airtight container.

Makes 14 biscuits

Gingerbread people

This is a great recipe to make with kids – they can do every step with minimal help and they really enjoy the decorating. Of course, best of all is the eating. Do you bite the arms off first? Or the head? Start at the knees please. Before you start, make sure you have a gingerbread person cookie cutter.

125 g dairy-free spread

60 g (¼ cup) brown sugar

90 g (¼ cup) molasses

1 teaspoon vanilla extract

450 g (2½ cups) wholemeal flour

½ teaspoon bicarbonate of soda

pinch of salt

1½ teaspoons ground ginger

1 teaspoon ground cinnamon

½ teaspoon ground nutmeg

pinch of ground cloves

VEGAN

Beat the dairy-free spread and sugar in a large mixing bowl using a wooden spoon or an electric mixer until creamy. Add the molasses, 3 tablespoons of water and vanilla and mix. Add the flour, bicarbonate of soda, salt, ginger, cinnamon, nutmeg and cloves and mix to form a rough dough.

Divide the dough into 2 pieces so it's easier to handle. Wrap each piece in plastic wrap and refrigerate for 1 hour.

Preheat the oven to 180°C. Grease and line 2 baking trays with greaseproof paper.

Place the first piece of dough between 2 sheets of greaseproof paper and roll out to a thickness of 2 cm. Use a cookie cutter to cut people shapes, arranging them on the baking trays.

Add any leftover dough to the second dough piece and roll it out between the 2 sheets of greaseproof paper. Continue cutting out people until all the dough is used.

Bake for 9–12 minutes, or until golden brown. Remove from the oven and transfer to wire racks to cool. The people should be ready for munching after about 20 minutes.

Store any leftover gingerbread people in an airtight container.

Makes 12 people

Spiced almond biscuits

I like to make these crispy little biscuits small enough to eat in one mouthful, but you can vary the size as you wish. I often make my own roasted almond butter, but it is easy to find in most supermarkets and health food stores.

200 g (2 cups) almond meal

120 g softened butter

100 g (½ cup) brown sugar

2 tablespoons Roasted Almond Butter (page 171)

1 teaspoon vanilla extract

1 teaspoon ground cinnamon

½ teaspoon ground nutmeg

pinch of salt

GLUTEN-FREE

Preheat the oven to 180°C. Line 2 baking trays with greaseproof paper.

In a large bowl combine all the ingredients and mix together with a wooden spoon or electric beater.

Shape the mixture into little balls about 3 cm in diameter. Place the balls on the trays and flatten slightly with your hand.

Bake for 12–15 minutes, or until golden. Place on wire racks to cool and crisp up. Store in an airtight container.

Makes 20 biscuits

Golden cinnamon shortbread

The first time I tried homemade shortbread I was 9. I was sitting beside my dad on a bus headed to Brisbane, and my brother was behind us, next to an older lady. I was thinking how lucky I was to score the seat next to Dad because he had a packet of Fantales in his bag. Then I heard the lady crack open a tin of homemade shortbread and the sound of my brother munching and laughing. She offered some to Dad and me and, oh my god, it was so delicious! The Fantales, of course, remained unopened until we got to Brisbane. This is my yummy vegan version of that shortbread.

250 g dairy-free spread
150 g (¾ cup) brown sugar
300 g (2 cups) plain flour, sifted
90 g (½ cup) rice flour
pinch of salt
pinch of ground cinnamon

VEGAN

Beat the dairy-free spread and sugar in a large bowl using a wooden spoon or an electric mixer until creamy. Fold in the flours, salt and cinnamon, stirring gently with a wooden spoon to form a rough dough.

Sprinkle some flour on a smooth, clean surface. Turn the dough out onto the floured surface and knead 10 times. (Don't overdo it. The less you handle the dough, the better your biscuits will be.) Divide the dough into two pieces and wrap each in plastic wrap. Refrigerate for 30 minutes.

Preheat the oven to 180°C. Grease and line 2 baking trays with greaseproof paper.

Place the first piece of dough on the floured surface and roll it out to make a pastry circle about 20 cm in diameter and 5 mm thick. Use the rolling pin to transfer the pastry to the baking tray. Repeat with the remaining dough portion and the other tray. Pinch the edges of the pastry for decoration. Use a knife to score the top of the pastry into 12 segments so it is easy to break once cooked.

Bake for 20 minutes until lightly golden. Allow to cool on the trays for a few minutes to firm up. Transfer to wire racks to cool completely.

Break or snap the biscuit circles along their cut marks. Store in an airtight container or jar.

Makes 24 biscuits

Vegan Anzac biscuits

This much-loved, traditional biscuit has been a staple in Australian and New Zealand homes for nearly 100 years. Do try this vegan version, and remember this is quite a large, crisp biscuit so it needs plenty of room to spread on the baking tray.

90 g (1 cup) rolled oats

150 g (1 cup) plain flour

90 g (1 cup) desiccated coconut

100 g (½ cup) brown sugar

125 g dairy-free spread, melted

2 tablespoons golden syrup

2 tablespoons blackstrap molasses

1 teaspoon bicarbonate of soda

VEGAN

Preheat the oven to 180°C. Grease and line 2 baking trays with greaseproof paper.

Place the oats, flour, coconut and sugar in a large bowl and mix well. Add the remaining ingredients and mix thoroughly to make a sticky dough.

With wet hands, roll tablespoons of the mixture into little balls. Place them on the baking trays, leaving room for spreading, and flatten slightly.

Bake for 12–15 minutes, or until golden brown. When you first take them out of the oven, the biscuits will be soft. Leave them to cool slightly on the trays before transferring them to a wire rack, where they will crisp up nicely.

Store in an airtight container.

Makes 20 biscuits

Little chocolate spud cakes

These amazing vegan cupcakes are moist, dense and *very* chocolatey. Decorated with icing sugar and raspberries, they are the perfect treat for a special afternoon tea.

145 g (1 cup) plain flour

1 tablespoon soy milk powder

40 g (⅓ cup) cocoa powder

¾ teaspoon bicarbonate of soda

190 g (2 cups) brown sugar

pinch of salt

100 g potato (about 1 large one), peeled and grated

60 g dairy-free spread, melted

250 ml (1 cup) almond milk (for a recipe, see page 234)

1 teaspoon vanilla extract

2 tablespoons icing sugar

125 g (1 punnet) raspberries

VEGAN

Preheat the oven to 180°C. Lightly grease a 12-hole muffin tin.

Sift the flour and soy milk powder into a large bowl. Use a fork to stir in the cocoa, bicarbonate of soda, sugar, salt and grated potato. Add the dairy-free spread, almond milk and vanilla. Mix with a wooden spoon until just combined – don't over-mix.

Pour the mixture into the 12 muffin holes and bake for 30 minutes, or until a skewer inserted in the centre of the cupcakes comes out clean.

Leave the cupcakes in the tin for 5 minutes before turning out onto a wire rack. Sift icing sugar over the top and decorate with raspberries.

Makes 12 small cakes

Lemon cake with almond butter icing

The citrus almond icing on this cake is divine. Feel free to use store-bought almond butter if you're not into making your own. Vegans can easily substitute the dairy-based ingredients with vegan alternatives.

125 g butter

100 g (½ cup) brown sugar

260 g (1 ¾ cups) self-raising flour

125 ml (½ cup) milk

1 tablespoon finely grated lemon zest

ICING

3 tablespoons caster sugar

3 tablespoons lemon juice

4 tablespoons Roasted Almond Butter (page 171)

Preheat the oven to 180°C. Grease a 20 cm round cake tin and line the base with greaseproof paper.

Cream the butter and sugar in a large bowl with a wooden spoon or electric mixer. When fluffy, add the milk and mix until well combined. Fold in the flour and lemon zest with a wooden spoon.

Pour the mixture into the cake tin and bake for 35 minutes, or until a skewer inserted in the centre of the cake comes out clean.

Leave the cake in the tin for 10 minutes before turning it out onto a wire rack. Allow to cool before icing.

To make the icing, combine the sugar and lemon juice in a small bowl. Stir in the almond butter to make a thick, smooth paste. Spread over the top of the cake.

Store the cake in an airtight container (refrigerate in summer).

Serves 8

Banana and walnut bread

This moist and light banana bread is wonderful fresh out of the oven, but is equally delicious cold or toasted and spread with almond butter.

100 g dairy-free spread

100 g (½ cup) brown sugar

120 ml (scant ½ cup) soy milk

3 teaspoons cornflour

3 ripe bananas, mashed

¼ cup walnuts, roughly chopped

300 g (2 cups) plain flour

1 teaspoon bicarbonate of soda

1 teaspoon baking powder

VEGAN

Preheat the oven to 180°C. Grease a loaf tin.

Use a wooden spoon or electric beater to cream the dairy-free spread and sugar in a large bowl until light and fluffy.

Whisk together 3 tablespoons of the soy milk and the cornflour in a small bowl to make an egg substitute. Add the mixture to the creamed butter and sugar and mix well. Stir in the banana, the remaining 3 tablespoons of soy milk and the walnuts. Mix well with a wooden spoon. Fold in the sifted flour, bicarbonate of soda and baking powder and mix gently until just combined.

Spoon the mixture into the prepared tin and bake for 45 minutes, or until a skewer inserted into the centre comes out clean.

Allow to cool in the tin for 5 minutes before transferring to a wire rack.

Serves 6–8

Full-on chocolate nut cake

The combination of smooth chocolate, roasted brazil nuts and zingy ginger makes this decadent treat perfect for a special occasion.

250 g dark dairy-free chocolate, roughly chopped

80 g (⅓ cup) dairy-free spread

3 tablespoons golden syrup

125 g (1 cup) slivered almonds

200 g (1¼ cups) brazil nuts, roughly chopped

135 g (1½ cups) desiccated coconut

50 g (¼ cup) glacé ginger

150 g (1 cup) currants

360 g (2½ cups) plain flour

60 g (½ cup) cocoa

1 teaspoon ground cinnamon

160 g (1½ cups) jam or marmalade

ICING

150 g dark dairy-free chocolate, roughly chopped

60 g dairy-free spread

VEGAN

Preheat the oven to 180°C. Grease the sides of a 30 cm low-sided tart tin with a removable base. Cut a circle of greaseproof paper to line the base.

Melt the chocolate and dairy-free spread in a small saucepan over a low heat, stirring often. When melted (about 10 minutes), stir in the golden syrup, almonds, brazil nuts and 3 tablespoons of water. Remove from the heat.

In a large bowl combine the coconut, ginger, currants, flour, cocoa, cinnamon and jam or marmalade. Pour in the melted chocolate mixture and stir well. Spoon the mixture into the baking tin and bake for 45 minutes, or until a skewer inserted in the centre comes out clean.

Remove the cake from the oven and allow to rest for 10 minutes. Run a butter knife around the edge of the cake and invert it onto a plate. Place a wire rack gently over the base of the cake and invert again so it's the right way up. Allow to cool.

To make the icing, melt the chocolate and dairy-free spread in a small saucepan over a low heat until melted (10–15 minutes). Allow the icing to cool for 10 minutes before spreading over the cake.

Serves 10

Chelsea buns

Pop the kettle on love, we're having Chelsea buns! These sweet, sticky delights take a bit of time, but they are worth it. Make sure you use real maple syrup to get the full flavour. I often bake a vegan version of the buns using egg replacer, soy milk and dairy-free spread.

600 g (4 cups) plain flour

¼ teaspoon mixed spice

½ teaspoon ground cinnamon

½ teaspoon ground nutmeg

1 tablespoon blackstrap molasses

2 eggs, whisked

3 tablespoons rice bran oil, plus extra for brushing

2½ tablespoons strawberry or raspberry jam

50 g (½ cup) roasted pecans, chopped

75 g (½ cup) currants

60 g (¼ cup) brown sugar

YEAST STARTER

2 sachets (14 g) or 2 teaspoons dry yeast

1 teaspoon brown sugar

375 ml (1½ cups) warm milk

1 teaspoon plain flour

ICING

185 g (1½ cups) icing sugar

2 tablespoons warm milk

1 tablespoon butter, melted

1 tablespoon maple syrup

To make the yeast starter, combine the yeast and brown sugar in a small mixing bowl. Stir in the warm milk and flour. Cover and leave in a warm spot for 15 minutes until the mixture becomes frothy.

Meanwhile, sift the flour into a large bowl. Add the mixed spice, cinnamon and nutmeg and stir gently with a wooden spoon. Add the molasses, eggs, oil and yeast starter and mix to form a rough dough. Turn the dough out onto the floured surface and knead for 5 minutes.

Rinse and dry the large bowl and grease it. Return the dough to the bowl, cover and stand it in a warm place for 1 hour, or until the dough has doubled in size.

Re-flour the smooth surface and grease 2 x 25 cm round cake tins. Tip the dough out onto the floured surface and knead for 3 minutes. Use a floured rolling pin to roll the dough into a 20 x 35 cm rectangle about 3 cm thick.

Brush the dough with rice bran oil. Gently spread jam over the dough leaving a 1 cm border around the edge. Evenly sprinkle over the pecans, currants and sugar and press in lightly. With the long edge closest to you, roll the dough into a lumpy sausage.

Cut the dough into 12 even pieces. Place 6 in each cake tin, jam swirls facing upwards. Cover and stand the rolls in a warm place for 40 minutes. (They will spread out in the tin and fill the gaps.)

Preheat the oven to 190°C.

Bake the buns for 30 minutes until they are golden brown and risen. Remove from the oven.

To make the icing, combine the icing sugar, milk and butter in a small bowl and mix well. Drizzle the icing and maple syrup over the buns while they are still warm. Let the buns cool in the tin for about 10 minutes before transferring them to wire racks. They'll be ready to enjoy with a cuppa after another 30 minutes. (You can store any leftovers in an airtight container for up to 2 days.)

Makes 12 buns

Chewy fruit and nut bars

These delicious, high-energy bars are great for outdoor adventures and brilliant for the kids' lunchboxes. Not only are they way cheaper than store-bought ones but also you know exactly what's in them.

80 g (½ cup) sesame seeds

60 g (½ cup) sunflower seeds

300 g (2 cups) almonds

pinch of salt

90 g (½ cup) dates, pitted and chopped

125 g (½ cup) raisins

90 g (½ cup) dried apricots, chopped

80 g (½ cup) dried figs, chopped

100 g (1 cup) rolled oats

100 g (5 cups) puffed rice

350 g (1 cup) rice malt syrup

375 g (1½ cups) crunchy peanut butter

115 g (1 cup) coconut milk powder

1 teaspoon vanilla extract

VEGAN

Preheat the oven to 160°C. Grease a slice tin and line the base with greaseproof paper.

Heat a frying pan over a medium heat and add the sesame seeds, sunflower seeds and almonds. Toast for 5 minutes, shaking or stirring them frequently so they don't burn, until they're browned and aromatic. Remove from the heat, sprinkle with salt and set aside to cool.

Place the dates, raisins, apricots and figs in a food processor. Add the toasted nuts and seeds. Pulse 2–3 times until the ingredients are finely chopped (not pureed). Transfer to a large bowl and stir in the oats and puffed rice.

Heat the rice malt syrup and peanut butter in a saucepan over a medium heat, stirring until well combined. When simmering, remove from the heat and stir in the coconut milk powder and vanilla extract. Pour the peanut syrup into the puffed rice mixture and use a wooden spoon to mix thoroughly.

Press the mixture into the prepared tin. Bake for 20–30 minutes, or until the top begins to brown slightly (the mixture will still be soft but not wet).

Cut into squares, and allow to cool completely before removing from the baking tin. Place in the fridge to harden and store in an airtight container.

Makes 16 bars

Homemade honeycomb (without the honey)

Please note that no bees were harmed in the making of this vegan treat! The syrupy sweetness comes not from honey, but from dark brown sugar, which contains more molasses than ordinary brown sugar. Use toothpicks to dip the honeycomb bites into melted dark chocolate, or just enjoy them as is.

210 g (1 cup) dark brown sugar

4 tablespoons golden syrup

3 teaspoons bicarbonate of soda

GLUTEN-FREE

VEGAN

Line a baking tray with greaseproof paper.

Melt the sugar, golden syrup and 1 tablespoon of water in a saucepan over a medium–low heat. Bring to the boil and cook for 10–15 minutes until the mixture darkens, thickens and begins to bubble all over. (To test if it is ready, drop a teaspoonful of the mixture into a bowl of cold water – if it turns solid you are ready to roll.)

Remove from the heat and quickly stir in the bicarbonate of soda. Use a spoon to scoop the mixture out of the pan and onto the greased baking tray.

Allow to cool at room temperature for at least 10 minutes then break it into bite-sized pieces. Place immediately in an airtight container, otherwise the sugar will melt and the outside will become sticky.

Makes about 300 g

Sunflower and paprika brittle

These gorgeous-looking sweet treats remind me of stained glass window fragments. You'll need a metal spatula and some cooking oil spray to make them. I use mild olive oil spray oil, but canola oil spray is also good.

125 g (1 cup) sunflower seeds

3 teaspoons paprika

pinch of salt

275 g (1¼ cups) sugar

2 tablespoons rice malt syrup

GLUTEN-FREE

VEGAN

Line a baking tray with greaseproof paper. Spray the paper with cooking oil spray. Spray a metal spatula with cooking oil spray and set aside for later.

Heat a large non-stick frying pan over a medium–high heat. Add the sunflower seeds and cook for 3 minutes, stirring often, until toasted and aromatic. Transfer the seeds to a large bowl and set aside.

Clean the frying pan with paper towel and return it to the heat. Add the paprika and immediately remove the pan from the heat. Stir the paprika so it doesn't burn but is aromatic. Transfer the paprika to the bowl of sunflower seeds, sprinkle with salt and mix well.

Place the sugar, rice malt syrup and 140 ml of water in a saucepan over a medium–high heat. Bring to a simmer, stirring often, until the sugar dissolves. Continue to cook, stirring constantly, for 3 minutes, or until you smell a hint of caramel.

Remove from the heat, quickly add the sunflower kernels and mix well. Use the oiled spatula to quickly spread the mixture onto the lined baking tray to a thickness of 3–4 mm.

Place in the fridge for 2 hours, or until completely cool. Peel the greaseproof paper away from the brittle (it should come away easily) and break the brittle into small pieces. Store in an airtight container (it will last for 2–3 weeks in the fridge).

Makes 230 g

Chia, coconut and strawberry popsicles

Healthy popsicles? It doesn't sound right, does it? But these are way more nutritious than any iced confection you can buy at the supermarket, and they look stunning. Give yourself plenty of time to make them as it takes 4 hours for the chia seeds to form a jelly and then they need to freeze for about 8 hours.

250 ml (1 cup) coconut milk

250 ml (1 cup) almond milk (for a recipe, see page 234)

280 g (1½ cups) strawberries, diced

4 tablespoons chia seeds

2 tablespoons desiccated coconut

55 g (¼ cup) raw sugar

GLUTEN-FREE

VEGAN

Place all the ingredients in a large bowl and mix well. Cover and refrigerate for 4 hours to allow the chia seeds to expand.

Pour the mixture into 8 × 250 ml popsicle (paddle pop) moulds and freeze overnight.

Makes 8 popsicles

Suzy's

Drinks

Pineapple and mint frappé

A glass of this freshly made frappé is the perfect summer drink – icy cold, fruity and with a hint of refreshing mint.

1 pineapple, peeled and chopped into large pieces

6 cups ice cubes

8 mint leaves

500 ml (2 cups) apple juice

GLUTEN-FREE

VEGAN

Combine all the ingredients in a blender and process until smooth. Serve immediately.

Serves 6–8

Incredible hulk juice

This juice is so healthy I swear it will give you superpowers. You don't need a juicer to make it, but you do need a blender or food processor and also some cheesecloth for straining.

6 kale leaves, de-stemmed and roughly chopped

4 granny smith apples, cored and diced

6 celery stalks, roughly chopped

4 cm piece of ginger, peeled

2 lemons, peeled and chopped

2 cucumbers, roughly chopped

500 ml (2 cups) chilled water

Place all the ingredients in a blender or food processer and blitz for 2 minutes, or until smooth.

Line a colander with a double layer of sterile cheesecloth. Place the colander over a bowl and pour in the juice. Stir with a spoon to help push the juice through. Draw the edges of the cheesecloth together and squeeze down to extract the remaining juice. Discard the pulp.

Transfer the juice to a clean jar or jug. Chill and serve with ice.

Serves 4

GLUTEN-FREE

VEGAN

Almond milk

Almond milk is another great milk substitute for vegans and people with lactose intolerance. It's naturally nutty, quite creamy and contains no cholesterol. Try making your own at home; it's much easier than you think. If you don't want to waste the pulp, you can use it to make almond cheese, biscuits or add it to porridge.

320 g (2 cups) almonds
2 dates, pitted
pinch of ground nutmeg
pinch of ground cinnamon
pinch of salt

GLUTEN-FREE

VEGAN

Place the almonds in a food processor and process on a medium speed for 2 minutes, or until finely ground. Add 500 ml (2 cups) of water and pulse for 1 minute. (Pulsing gives the mixture time to fall away from the sides back into the bowl – allowing you to use gravity to your advantage.) Add 1 litre (4 cups) of water and process for 3 minutes. Add the dates, nutmeg, cinnamon and salt and process for another 3 minutes.

Line a colander with sterile cheesecloth and set it over a large bowl. (The colander needs to fit just inside the rim so there is room below.)

Pour the almond mixture into the cheesecloth-lined colander. Stir it with a spoon so the milky liquid separates from the pulp and runs into the bowl. Draw the edges of the cheesecloth together and squeeze down to extract all the liquid.

Pour the almond milk into a jug or bottle, cover and refrigerate until cold. Almond milk will last for 4–5 days in an airtight container in the fridge.

Makes 1.5 litres

Rice milk

Rice milk is the most hypoallergenic of all the milk replacements because it's suitable for those with lactose intolerance, gluten intolerance and nut allergies. It's delicious on breakfast cereal, excellent for cooking, makes great smoothies, and is full of essential nutrients and vitamins. You can easily experiment with other sweeteners such as dates, prunes, figs or cane sugar; or leave out the sweetener altogether.

440 g (2 cups) brown rice

90 g (¼ cup) rice malt syrup

2 tablespoons vanilla extract

pinch of salt

GLUTEN-FREE

VEGAN

Place the rice in a large bowl with 1.5 litres of water. Cover and leave in the fridge for 12 hours or overnight.

Pour the soaked rice into a blender or food processor. Add the rice malt syrup, vanilla and salt and process for 2 minutes, or until smooth and creamy.

Line a colander with sterile cheesecloth and place it over a large bowl so that it just fits and leaves some space underneath. Pour the rice mixture into the cheesecloth. Stir it with a spoon so the milk separates from the pulp and runs into the bowl. Draw the edges of the cheesecloth together and squeeze down to extract all the remaining rice milk. Discard the pulp.

Pour the rice milk into a jug with a lid or cover with plastic wrap. Refrigerate until cold. Consume within 2–3 days.

Makes 1.5 litres

Oat milk

Oat milk is a wonderful substitute for cow's milk, so is perfect for vegans and anyone with lactose intolerance. Some people who are gluten-intolerant can eat oats. Oats are high in protein, iron and B vitamins. Steel-cut oats are simply whole-grain oats that have been cut into a couple of pieces instead of being rolled flat. These can be bought at almost any supermarket and all health food stores. Feel free to experiment with different sweeteners such as brown sugar, dates, figs, brown rice syrup or stevia.

160 g (2 cups) steel-cut oats
1.5 litres hot water
3 tablespoons golden syrup
1 tablespoon vanilla extract
pinch of salt

VEGAN

Place the oats and water in a large bowl, cover and set aside to soak for 2 hours.

Line a colander with sterile cheesecloth and set it over another large bowl so that it just fits and leaves some space underneath.

Pour the oats and water into a food processer. Add the golden syrup, vanilla extract and salt and process for 2 minutes. Pour the mixture into the cheesecloth-lined colander. Stir it with a spoon so the milky liquid separates from the pulp and runs into the bowl. Draw the edges of the cheesecloth together and squeeze down with your hands to extract all the oat milk. Discard the pulp (or save it to make a cake or slice, or dry it and use it for muesli).

Pour the oat milk into a jug with a lid if you have one, if not just cover with plastic wrap and refrigerate until cold. Oat milk will last for 3–4 days in a sealed container in the fridge.

Makes 1.5 litres

Lemon, ginger and barley water

This delicious drink was traditionally given to invalids to boost their immune systems. Nowadays it is enjoyed as a refreshing hit of antioxidants and energy. The discarded barley may be added to dried fruit and nuts and served with soy or almond milk for breakfast.

220 g (1 cup) pearl barley, rinsed

2 slices of ginger

zest and juice of 2 lemons

110 g (½ cup) sugar

2 tablespoons molasses

VEGAN

Place the barley, ginger and lemon zest in a large saucepan with 1.5 litres of water. Bring to the boil over a medium heat. Reduce the heat and simmer for 15 minutes. Strain over a heatproof bowl, discarding the barley (or saving for breakfast). Add the sugar and molasses to the bowl and stir to dissolve. Allow the barley water to cool slightly then stir in the lemon juice.

Pour into a bottle or jug with a lid and refrigerate. Drink when cold. Use within 4 days.

Makes 1.5 litres

Soy milk chai

This delicious hot drink is spicy, fragrant and deservedly popular.

4 cm piece of ginger, finely sliced

6 cardamom pods, cracked

3 star-anise

2 cinnamon sticks

3 teaspoons earl grey tea leaves

2 black peppercorns

3 cloves

1.25 litres soy milk

GLUTEN-FREE

VEGAN

In a large saucepan combine all the ingredients with 500 ml (2 cups) of water. Bring to the boil then reduce the heat and simmer for 20 minutes.

Strain and serve with or without sugar (I like a spoonful of brown sugar in mine).

Serves 6

Christmas snog

This is a lot like a vegan version of eggnog, but you don't need to wait for Christmas to enjoy it! Sip it on a cold winter's night, wrapped in a doona, watching your favourite movie. You can make your own almond milk, or buy some at any supermarket or health food store.

1 litre (4 cups) almond milk (for a recipe, see page 234)

3 tablespoons golden syrup

1 teaspoon vanilla extract

2 teaspoons brandy extract or 2½ tablespoons brandy

1 teaspoon ground nutmeg

1 teaspoon ground cinnamon

1 teaspoon ground ginger

1 cinnamon stick

3 slices of ginger

Place all the ingredients in a large saucepan over a medium heat. Heat gently for 10 minutes, stirring often. Do not boil. If a skin forms on the surface, scoop it off and discard it.

Serve hot in mugs.

Serves 4

GLUTEN-FREE

VEGAN

Mulled apple cider

One of the many generous souls who volunteered to test my recipes sent me an email after receiving this one with the query, 'So when do I add the mull?' Bless him! Enjoy this cider on a cold winter's night or in the great outdoors by a campfire. If you have a juicer, you can make your own fresh apple juice. If not, store-bought cloudy apple juice will be fine.

juice of 16 sweet apples (about 1 litre, or 4 cups)

juice of 1 large lemon

juice of 1 orange

3 tablespoons raw sugar

1 tablespoon julienned orange rind

1½ teaspoons ground allspice

3 cloves

3 cinnamon sticks

2 teaspoons ground nutmeg

2 peppercorns

GLUTEN-FREE

VEGAN

Place all the ingredients in a large saucepan. Bring to the boil, then reduce the heat to low and simmer for 20 minutes. Strain before serving.

You can serve this mulled cider hot, but it's just as delicious chilled. Store it in the fridge in a jug or container with a lid – it will keep for 3–4 days.

Serves 4

Suzy says

Thank you

Thank you to everyone who has contributed to the making of this book. It has definitely been a team effort.

Thanks to Mary Small for being the greatest publisher and driving force behind this project; Jane Winning, for expertly wrangling all parts of the process and working closely with me to turn an idea and a bunch of recipes into this amazing book; and editor Miriam Cannell for turning my scribblings into sentences and making it all make sense. To Michelle Mackintosh for making the book look so beautiful; and to Pauline Haas, for such skilled typesetting. Thanks to Lucy Malouf, Jo Rudd and Tom Saras. Special thanks to the very talented photographer Steve Brown and the gifted stylist Kristine Duran-Thiessen for making the food look so lovely and for making the photo shoot a truly enjoyable experience that I will never forget. And thanks to my good friend Popcorn Oscar-Chemello for helping me prepare the food for the shoot, and for teaching me to work in a professional kitchen all those years ago. Thanks to all the people who helped test the recipes over the years, with special thanks to Annette Schwanke and Runa Saari for their cooking expertise. Thanks to my Mum, Dad and family for their love and support. And the biggest thanks to my darling partner, Tracy Smith, for putting up with me and being the best partner I could ever wish for.

Suzy's recipe

Index

A PLUM BOOK

First published in 2014 by
Pan Macmillan Australia Pty Limited
Level 25, 1 Market Street
Sydney NSW 2000, Australia

Level 1, 15–19 Claremont Street
South Yarra Victoria 3141, Australia

Design by Michelle Mackintosh
Photography by Steve Brown
Prop and food styling by Kristine Duran-Thiessen
Cover photography by Mark Roper
Cover styling by Karina Duncan
Food preparation by Suzy Spoon and
Popcorn Oscar-Chemello
Cover food preparation by Emma Warren
Edited by Miriam Cannell
Typeset by Pauline Haas
Index by Jo Rudd
Colour reproduction by Splitting Image Colour Studio
Printed and bound in China by 1010 Printing
International Limited

A CIP catalogue record for this book is available from the
National Library of Australia.

The publisher would like to thank the following for their
generosity in providing props for the book: Southwood,
AURA by Tracie Ellis, Mud Australia, Marie-Helene
Clauzon, Freedom Furniture and Homewares, Porter's
Paint, Have You Met Miss Jones and Dinosaur Designs.

10 9 8 7 6 5 4 3 2 1